SHE LOVED

Resting in the Beauty of Motherhood

SUZANNE BILODEAU

ASCENSION
West Chester, Pennsylvania

© 2025 Ascension Publishing Group, LLC. All rights reserved.

With the exception of short excerpts used in articles and critical reviews, no part of this work may be reproduced, transmitted, or stored in any form whatsoever, printed or electronic, without the prior written permission of the publisher.

Excerpts from the English translation of the *Catechism of the Catholic Church* for use in the United States of America © 1994, 1997 by the United States Catholic Conference, Inc.–Libreria Editrice Vaticana. Used by permission. All rights reserved.

Unless otherwise noted, Scripture passages are from the Revised Standard Version–Second Catholic Edition © 2006 by the Division of Christian Education of the National Council of the Churches of Christ in the United States of America. Used by permission. All rights reserved.

Scripture texts marked "NAB" in this work are taken from the New American Bible, revised edition © 2010, 1991, 1986, 1970 Confraternity of Christian Doctrine, Washington, DC, and are used by permission of the copyright owner. All rights reserved. No part of the New American Bible may be reproduced in any form without permission in writing from the copyright owner.

"Litany for Motherhood" by Marie Loesel. Used by permission.

Ascension
PO Box 1990
West Chester, PA 19380
1-800-376-0520
ascensionpress.com

Design by Ashley Dias

Author photography by Elizabeth Wertz (p. iv)
Cover and Interior Photography: Adobe Stock

Printed in China
25 26 27 28 29 5 4 3 2 1

ISBN 978-1-935940-41-8

*In the twilight of life,
God will not judge us on our
earthly possessions and human successes,
but on how well we have loved.*

Attributed to

- *St. John of the Cross* -

Dedication

For the six little souls that call me "Momma." Madelyn, Noah, Jean-David, Bernadette, Colette, and Brigitte, thank you for being the most beautiful and unexpected place that I have encountered Christ. You have stretched me, taught me, and loved me. Your squishy hands, curious eyes, and unbridled hearts have shown me what it means to be free and alive in Christ's love. Regardless of how clean the house is, how fresh the meals are, or how frequently I am in sweats, you have showered me with an undeserving and restoring love. It is through my motherhood to you, that God is good to his promises "I will give you a new heart and put a new spirit in you. I will remove from you your heart of stone and give you a heart of flesh" (Ezekiel 36:26). I can only pray that my love for you will be but a mere foretaste of the love that your Heavenly Father has for you.

Table of Contents

Foreword *by Dr. Bob Schuchts* ix
Introduction: A Mother's Love *by Suzanne Bilodeau* 1
Moving Through This Book (*A Note to the Reader*) 11

Letters by Catholic Mothers to Their Younger Selves

LOVE IS PATIENT 15
"Dear Younger Mom" *by Alicia Hernon* 21

LOVE IS KIND 31
"Hello, Darling Younger Self" *by Heidi Bratton* 37

LOVE DOES NOT ENVY 49
"Dear Sweet Mama" *by Heather Voccola* 57

LOVE IS NOT BOASTFUL 67
"Dear Precious Mama" *by Dorothy Pilarski* 75

LOVE IS NOT PROUD 89
"Dear Younger Self" *by Emily Jaminet* 95

LOVE HONORS OTHERS 107
"Hello, Love" *by Lisa Brenninkmeyer* 113

LOVE DOES NOT INSIST ON ITS OWN WAY 127
"Hey, Sweet Girl!" *by Elizabeth Foss* 133

LOVE DOES NOT BECOME ANGRY EASILY 145
　"Dear Younger Self" *by Christine Dudley* 153

LOVE DOES NOT KEEP A RECORD OF WRONGS 163
　"Dear Younger Me" *by Beth Sri* 169

**LOVE DOES NOT DELIGHT IN EVIL,
BUT REJOICES IN TRUTH** 181
　"Dear Younger Self" *by Carrie Daunt* 189

LOVE BEARS ALL THINGS 197
　"Hey, Super Mom!" *by Laura Phelps* 203

LOVE BELIEVES ALL THINGS 213
　"Dear Younger Self" *by Christine Hanus* 219

LOVE HOPES ALL THINGS 231
　"To My Younger Self" *by Debbie Herbeck* 237

LOVE ENDURES ALL THINGS 251
　"Dear Younger Me" *by Bonnie Landry* 257

LOVE NEVER FAILS 267
　"Hey Sis" *by Mary Lenaburg* 273

One More Note 287
Litany for Motherhood *by Marie Loesel* 289
Acknowledgments 291
Notes 293
Bibliography 294
More About Us 295

Foreword

BY DR. BOB SCHUCHTS

I am convinced that being a mom is one of the greatest and most essential vocations in the world. In his *Letter to Families*, St. John Paul II asserts that mothers and fathers are the icons of God and serve as the most fundamental building blocks of society. He goes on to say that there is no greater communion on earth than that between a mother and a child. The psychological and physical well-being of every child is essentially dependent on good mothering, beginning in the womb. Along with the love of a father who is present to his child, this bond with a mother is essential to the growth and development of each precious child. Yet, as every mother knows, there is nothing more challenging than being an attentive and loving mom. It requires every fiber of your being and constantly tests your capacity to love.

Jesus, who is love incarnate, grew up in a family, where he received the tenderness of his mother, Mary, and his foster father, Joseph. The Blessed Mother is the archetype and exemplar of Motherhood. She went through many painful moments in her motherhood, but Mary, who was "full of grace," could love through them all. The rest of us have not yet been perfected in love. And that is why this book is so necessary and likewise so beautiful.

A caring mom imitates Jesus' depth of self-giving love, the kind of love that welled from his mother. There is no greater love than laying down your life for another (see John 15:13). And that's what moms do every day for their children. With Jesus, every mom can say: "This is my body which is given for you" (Luke 22:19).

Despite these realities, our culture has continued to devalue the role of motherhood. In the early part of the twentieth century, Margaret Sanger, the founder of Planned Parenthood, rejected motherhood, marriage, and religion in the name of freedom for women. We have seen the fruit of those ideas in the second half of the twentieth century until the present day. In the 1960s and 70s, radical feminists asserted that mothers should not be permitted to bond with their children, in order not to be limited in their professional careers, positing that a woman only had worth if she could make a lot of money and find a prestigious career. Today, many are fighting to eliminate the word "mother" and have even proposed laws to forbid anyone calling someone a mother. What lunacy!

I remember when my daughters Carrie and Kristen were in middle school. When their classmates asked my daughters what they wanted to be when they grew up, they both said, "To get

"This is my body
which is given for you"
(Luke 22:19).

married and be a mom." The other kids mocked them. Sadly, all the students were being indoctrinated into the radical feminist agenda.

As a dad, it hurt my heart to hear my daughters' pure and holy desires being attacked. My daughters were not against careers in the workplace, but they understood that these careers were subordinate to the vocation of being a wife and mom. Their mother, a caring and capable labor and delivery nurse, had always placed being a mom above her career, making many sacrifices along the way.

In my work as a marriage and family therapist and teacher of human development for many years, I knew without any question that loving moms and dads are essential to every child's well-being. But you don't need a degree to know this. It is common sense, and every sane person knows this to be true. Despite the delusions of our culture, there is no replacement for a good mom. That is why I am excited for every mom to receive this beautiful book by Suzanne Bilodeau.

It's been a delight to read through this book and to see it come to fruition. I know that many women will be deeply blessed by it. And it will bear great fruit in the lives of their husbands and children and in the women they influence. The theme of the book is brilliant. It is older moms writing to their younger selves, giving them advice from what they have learned over the years about being a mother. You may recognize the names of several of the women who have written the letters in various chapters,

as some of them are involved in women's ministry—including my daughter Carrie.

I met Suzanne several years ago at a daily Mass in Michigan (where my team and I were offering a Healing the Whole Person Conference). I looked across the aisle and noticed a radiant pregnant woman. Throughout the Mass, I felt inspired to pray for her and for the precious baby she was carrying in her womb. Without knowing why, I also felt prompted to meet her, but she left church before I could get over to her pew. I wondered why, with all the people at daily Mass, I was being drawn to meet this woman. The next day someone I had met a few years earlier sought me out to introduce me to her sister. When I saw that I was being introduced to the pregnant woman from the day before, I had to smile. I didn't have to introduce myself. God had providentially prepared the way.

Most of my interactions with Suzanne over the past several years concern the subject of healing and motherhood. Even that first day, when I met her, I heard how deeply she desired to be a loving mom. This book has been conceived in her own prayer, for you to be the best mom you can be for your children.

The book is organized around the great passage about love in St. Paul's letter to the Corinthians (see 1 Corinthians 13: 4–8). As you prepare to read through this book, I encourage you to reflect on these words, which are read at many weddings:

- Read through the verses slowly, three times. The first time, every time the word love is mentioned, put Mary's name in the place of "love." For example: "Mary is patient, Mary is kind." This is a portrait of motherly love, perfected by grace.
- As you read these verses the second time, put your own name each time the word love appears: "I am patient, I am kind …" Notice how you feel this time. Notice that these words are true at times, but also notice the inadequacy you feel at times when you lack patience and kindness, and all the attributes of love. It is exactly in those places that this book will be a great consolation and a source of wisdom and encouragement for you. Suzanne and each of the women write with compassion and mercy in the areas where love is not yet perfected.
- Finally, read through the love passage a third time, and put in your name along with the Holy Spirit. "The Holy Spirit within me is patient. The Holy Spirit within me is kind." Do you notice the difference? This is the secret of Mary's motherhood. She, who was "full of grace," lived in complete dependence on the Holy Spirit. This is the key to your motherhood: ask the Holy Spirit for assistance, in imitation of Mary. Then, be patient and kind to yourself, as the first two chapters will encourage.

As you read this book, you will see that other mothers share in your frustrations, joys, shortcomings, and hope. No matter what age you are, you will be able to look back at earlier years and see your growth. As women you are journeying together as sisters, walking toward the Source of All Love!

I am praying for you! More importantly, Mary, our Mother, is praying for you, along with St. Joseph, and all the saints, through the Holy Spirit! May this book deeply bless and encourage you and refresh your motherly heart.

DR. BOB SCHUCHTS

Founder of the John Paul II Healing Center

A Mother's Love

You are rewarded not according to your work or your time but according to the measure of your love.

ST. CATHERINE OF SIENA

Oh, this thing we call *motherhood*. What woman fully understands this beautiful and sanctifying vocation, even as she gazes into tiny eyes that look to her as the guiding compass toward beauty, goodness, and truth? Yet, millions of mothers wake up every day, often disheveled and exhausted, to tend once again to the needs of little hearts and minds and bodies.

Maybe you are sipping your tea or coffee flipping through the pages of this book while your children run wild in the yard on a sunny day. Maybe you are juggling your baby on your hip while you try to squeeze in just a few sentences at a time. Or perhaps it is late into the night, you just finished consoling a pre-teen heart, and you have finally collapsed onto the couch with a glass of wine and this book. Regardless of your day, your location, or your season, there is a unique connection that exists among feminine hearts. Women all over the world are nursing babies, changing diapers, kissing boo-boos, wiping tears, cooking meals, folding clothes, and moving forward just one tiny step at a time on this journey of motherhood.

THE MAGNIFICENT CHALLENGE OF MOTHERHOOD

Lost among the dishes and laundry and busy amid the spilled milk and muddy footprints, many of us lose sight of the profound and eternal impact of our motherhood. Our culture, which praises worldly success and gain, quietly dismisses the heroic gift of a mother's body, heart, and soul. Yet, women everywhere play an often hidden yet magnificent role in God's story of salvation. Venerable Cardinal József Mindszenty emphasizes the immeasurable importance of a mother:

> The Most Important Person on earth is a mother. She cannot claim the honor of having built Notre Dame Cathedral. She need not. She has built something more magnificent than any cathedral—a dwelling for an immortal soul, the tiny perfection of her baby's body. The angels have not been blessed with such a grace. They cannot share in God's creative miracle to bring new saints to Heaven. Only a human mother can. Mothers are closer to God the Creator than any other creature; God joins forces with mothers in performing this act of creation. What on God's good earth is more glorious than this: to be a mother?[1]

For years now, I have prayed through what it means to step into this most divinely appointed role of shepherding little hearts—

motherhood. Like most women, my heart is consumed with a desire to love my children well. This desire is something divinely infused into the hearts of all mothers. In fact, God placed this desire into our hearts as directly as he put the blood within our veins. And if God placed the desire here, then it must be in his will to fulfill it. Yet, we often feel unequipped and unsure how we are to participate in this divine plan.

In the earliest years, I often found myself consumed with following the "how-tos" laid out by many books and speakers. I yearn for my kids to know the highest *perfection*—the heart of God; a God who intimately and personally sees them, knows them, and loves them. But how can I best do this? Is the answer found in the perfect apple pie recipe or the most organized home? Will I discover the secret if I count the number of activities they are involved in or add up how many friends they have? Is the answer found by ensuring they are quiet in church or able to pass all of their catechesis questions with ease and joy? No, I've swiftly learned that this vocation was never meant to fit a box or a tightly knit-together formula. Trust me, as a former actuary I've tried and found that there are no math equations that can craft your motherhood.

Instead, just as paragraph 25 of the *Catechism of the Catholic Church* emphasizes that "the whole concern of doctrine and its teaching must be directed to the love that never ends," so too the whole concern of motherhood must be directed to the love that never ends. "The love of our Lord must always be made accessible, so that anyone can see that all the works of perfect

Christian virtue spring from love and have no other objective than to *arrive at love*" (CCC 25, emphasis added).

WHERE LOVE LEADS

Sure, we all instinctively desire to love well, but what if the key to responding to this God-given desire is to realize that it is a call to something beyond ourselves? We mothers have a hunger to feast on the harvest we are gathering through the many years of laying our lives down for the souls in our homes. We want to taste the fruit of our labor; to give our children security in our imperfect love. We spend endless days watering the garden and plucking the weeds. But what if our flowers weren't meant to merely grow for a season, but rather nurtured on fertile ground to thrive for eternity? What if we aren't meant to lead them merely to something good, but rather to something great, or better yet, something perfect?

The truth is that our maternal love was designed to lead our children toward *Love*, himself (see 1 John 4:8). God most perfectly crafted the heart of a mother to be an instrument of love that leads his children into his waiting arms.

So if our greatest objective is to arrive at love, how do we do this? It begins by understanding what God, who is Love himself, says love is. Our Lord speaks through St. Paul in 1 Corinthians 13:4–8 when he so beautifully lays out the many facets of love. So beautifully in fact, that I found myself weeping before Jesus in the Blessed Sacrament as I prayed through these profound and yet simple words found in Sacred Scripture.

Love is patient and kind;
love is not jealous or boastful;
it is not arrogant or rude.
Love does not insist on its own way;
it is not irritable or resentful;
it does not rejoice at wrong,
but rejoices in the right.
Love bears all things, believes all things,
hopes all things, endures all things.
Love never ends.
–1 Corinthians 13:4–8

These few Bible passages will be the framework, outline, and backbone of this book. I hope that through a deeper understanding of these words, we may be guided in love and toward love resulting in a motherhood that abounds with a love that only the grace of God himself can produce.

WHO CAN SHOW US HOW?

To explore the many ingredients that God says love contains, I have enlisted some of our big sisters in Christ to share their experiences of love and motherhood. If you are looking for carefully laid out instructions on the five best ways to keep a tidy home or the three best strategies for disciplining your children, this is not the book for you. Instead, this book is a collective of unguarded and unbridled words written as **letters from mothers to their younger selves**. As they reflect on the words of 1 Corinthians 13, they speak of their journeys of persevering in love through the messy and beautiful, the pain and joy, the regrets and triumphs.

The vulnerable and encouraging words from women alongside, further along, or near the summit of this motherhood trail—a trail they walked, stumbled along, and blazed—may just lead us to the sustaining hope we need.

We spend countless hours and years learning the ways of mathematics, how to write a good paper, and the steps to build a glowing resume fit for a king. Yet, little time is spent training the souls of women so we can walk hand in hand with little ones. For most of mankind's history, over thousands of years, women have been shepherded into motherhood. Yet, with the busyness of our modern world, a vital piece of our humanity has been lost. We no longer sit around a village square or one-room home with wise women teaching us how to train up our children in love.

We all know the saying "It takes a village to raise a child." We often use this phrase—jokingly or seriously—when we could use the physical help of childcare or meals made. Yet, the deeper importance found hiding behind these eight words is the wisdom, experience, and encouragement that a *village* provides young mothers. God laid out his perfect design when he ordered community and shepherding as a way of life. "Two are better than one, because they have a good reward for their toil. For if they fall, one will lift up his fellow; but woe to him who is alone when he falls and has not another to lift him up" (Ecclesiastes 4:9–10). When we fall face forward into our bed full of tears of regret over a lost temper or tears of compassion for the heartache of a lonely child, who will be there to encourage our hearts? Who will remind us to persevere in beauty and goodness? It likely won't be our hired babysitter or the meal delivery driver. No, instead the vulnerable and encouraging words from women alongside, further along, or near the summit of this motherhood trail—a trail they walked, stumbled along, and blazed—may just lead us to the sustaining hope we need.

WITNESSES OF LOVE

I once shed tears to my spiritual director about my ferocious desire to walk hand-in-hand with wise, loving, and experienced women and men who could shepherd my heart toward love. I felt lost and concerned that this desire conflicted with my trusting relationship with Christ. Shouldn't my relationship with Momma Mary and God the Father himself be enough to sustain me? My spiritual director's short answer was, "Yes, *however*, in his perfect order, God, who entered the world through a family, designed us so that his loving character and heart would be mediated through the flesh of a mother and father." No, he did not think my desire was disordered at all. Rather, it makes perfect sense that we seek to learn the ways of love through other people; people who are living witnesses and vessels of God's love.

For many, this witness of God's love wasn't always shared and on display within the walls of our own homes. So we can become lost sheep, searching for the words and experiences of others to help shepherd our hearts in love. But God doesn't want to leave us wandering, lost, and afraid. Instead, he wants to lead us in love just as he has similarly called us to help usher our children in love. And maybe one of the ways God wants to lead us is through the hearts of others. In their own motherhood walk with Jesus, women have gained wisdom and learned lessons that could both encourage and guide their younger sisters in Christ.

So this has become my mission—to learn from women who have journeyed through motherhood—who have cried and laughed, who have been steadfast and stretched, who have fallen and gotten back up again. I do not want to simply watch Instagram reels or read how-to books on the best practices of motherhood. No, I'm not seeking women who look perfect or think they have loved perfectly, but rather those who desire to love well through knowing *Love* himself. I want to learn from the many women who embrace the calling of Titus 2:3–4: "They are to *teach* what is good, and so *train the young women to love* their husbands and children" (emphasis added).

THE MISSION OF MOTHERHOOD

Through the wisdom of mothers who walk beside us and have gone before us, I hope the fiery desire to love will be reignited and set ablaze within the hearts of many. Though leaving behind a legacy of love is a beautiful and noble desire, we must remember that loving well should never be the end goal. Instead, loving well is just one of the beautiful conduits that Love himself uses to draw his children back to him.

And my friends, this is why I desire to learn the ways of love. At the end of this short life here on earth, I do not desire for any accolades to be written in my obituary. It need not say things like, "She was a great homeschooler," or "She kept a tidy home." No, I hope that I can earn the honor of having two simple words laid out upon my gravestone: **She Loved**, and this book is one part of my mission of finding out how.

This book is an intimate exploration and uncovering of what it means to love. Through the vulnerable words of others, it will provide you with access to some of the most powerful lessons learned and intimate experiences shared. As you read through the pages, it is my hope that you will feel seen, known, and encouraged. I pray that the solidarity unearthed amongst the letters will reignite your heart with the profound and eternal mission of your motherhood.

SUZANNE BILODEAU

Moving Through This Book

A NOTE TO THE READER

Dear Reader,

As you move through this book and read the words of these mothers, I want to note one thing. These pages are not meant to be carefully scripted and crafted advice. My great desire was that the words would pour out from the depths of these women's hearts. Therefore, it was very important to the mission of this book that each woman spend time with our Lord in prayer and reflection to explore and share the lessons she has learned about love on her way. To access the more intimate and vulnerable corners of her heart, the corners that have the greatest capacity to encourage and strengthen our own missions, I have asked each woman to compose **a letter** as if she were writing it to her *younger mother self*. "From the depth of your own heart, what would you say to your younger self if you could? What would you want her to know?" These are the questions I asked, and this book is their answer.

Each chapter begins with a quote from those whose lives themselves were a living witness of love—the saints. Following each quote, I introduce the specific area of love we are exploring as outlined by 1 Corinthians 13, followed by an intimate letter written by a mother, often with tears in her eyes, to her younger self.

This book is not meant to be swallowed up in one big swoop of the eyes. Instead, I invite you to move through the pages of this book with a slow grace and allow the words to find their way into the home of your heart. Let our Lord reach into those weary, fearful, confused, or seeking places of your gloriously crafted momma soul, one intimate letter at a time. Pause, pray, reflect. Let him reveal the raw places that he desires to meet you and press his finger into the sacred story of your own motherhood. Let him remind you—his magnificent workmate—of his kindness, his mercy, your belovedness, and your chosenness. It is my prayer that through the letters in this book, the Lord will help you begin releasing the chains of perfectionism, unworthiness, and comparison. Let God unveil the masterpiece of his love that has been carefully sewn into the unique tapestry of your vocation. Then you, sweet momma, will find yourself **resting in the beauty of motherhood.**

- SHE LOVED -

Love is patient and kind;
love is not jealous or boastful;
it is not arrogant or rude.
Love does not insist on its own way;
it is not irritable or resentful;
it does not rejoice at wrong,
but rejoices in the right.
Love bears all things,
believes all things,
hopes all things,
endures all things.
Love never ends.

1 Corinthians 13:4-8

Love Is Patient

Have patience with all the world,
but first of all with yourself.

ST. FRANCIS DE SALES

It must have been the obvious dust blanketing the picture frame that made my spiritual director pause and wink at me. "I'm guessing that you don't change this very often," Father said with a chuckle. My spiritual director was right. This eight-by-eleven paper that had been framed and hung on our kitchen wall had remained the same for over two years. Yet, when I originally began hanging a 'Virtue of the Month,' I had every intention of mastering the virtue as a family and replacing it with a new word every month. In fact, we thought we had made some progress with many of the virtues we hung, such as *humility, fortitude, honesty,* and *temperance*. However, when it came time to tackle patience, something slowed down. Our progress halted. Maybe I got lazy and inconsistent with my attempts to rally the troops and grow in virtue, or maybe, and more likely, this momma deeply lacked the virtue on display and didn't know where to start.

Though I have not yet mastered the virtues and fall short of fully embodying the love of Christ, one thing I do know is that my role as mother to these little people in my home is a monumental part of God's story of salvation. In fact, every woman who gently swaddles her baby, ties the shoes of her toddler, cleans up the explosion left behind by tiny hands and feet, or tends to the activities and hearts of her growing children has been uniquely and profoundly ordained by God as a collaborator of love. And it is through this unparalleled maternal love that our Lord desires to accomplish his divine plans of encompassing the world, and specifically our own children, with his most perfect love. With God, we are on mission. But we determined and good-willed mothers often forget that missions are not frequently accomplished overnight; in fact, the *Catechism of the Catholic Church* reminds us that "missionary endeavor requires *patience*" (CCC 854, original emphasis).

*Be patient with a mission, with **this** mission? How can we be?* we ask ourselves.

My role as mother to these little people in my home is a monumental part of God's story of salvation.

I've lost my temper and yelled for the eighteenth time today, the kids fail to listen, the house is a mess, and once again this weary momma hid in a corner to cry hot and heavy tears. How can I be patient when my mission field looks like this? Deep in the mess, we struggle to see the fruit of our maternal love or the growth in the hearts of our children. So we become wary of showing up for the battle of love, let go of our ideals, and turn away from the heights of God's call.

But what if one little seed could bring our labor of love into full view? Like the love and virtue in our hearts and homes, wild leek does not grow overnight. In fact, the ramp seed of the wild leek can take a whole year before it begins to germinate.² Above the surface, you can water, tend, and weed for the good of the seed below for hundreds of days, and yet you would never see any progress. To "toil by the sweat of your brow" without any sign of growth would likely discourage many of us. Then, even after the plant has begun to grow above the surface, it can take seven years before it begins to flower and produce fruit. With no beauty in sight, many of us may be tempted to walk away hopeless and depleted. Yet, unbeknownst to many impatient gardeners, the plant's growth in strength and maturation is gentle and unhurried. Then miraculously, one day, after potentially thousands of days of waiting, the flower blooms, and shortly after, the fruit emerges.³

What if the maturation of our own love and the development of character in our children are similarly growing in strength and virtue over time, which we cannot easily see above the surface? What if our weary eyes, which are often focused on digging up the weeds of our days, miss seeing the slow and gentle emerging "fruit" of our labor? Lucky for us, our King has a full view of everything above the surface, below, and in between. He sees the growth and is actively participating in the outstretching and expanding nature of our hearts and theirs. He is working out the story of our lives if only we patiently trust in this glorious book he is writing. St. Paul reminds us of the holy patience of waiting. "If we hope for what we do not see, we wait for it with *patience*" (Romans 8:25, emphasis added).

Joseph in the Old Testament shows us the treasure of holy waiting. Kidnapped and sold into slavery by his own brothers,

Joseph, only seventeen years old, could not have seen what God was accomplishing with his robbed and fractured life. Yet, he was patient. Falsely accused of wrongdoing by his master's wife and thrown into jail, Joseph remained patient. In fact, he endured thirteen years of brutal hardship before God revealed the fruit of Joseph's hidden and trustful life by leading him into the companionship of the Pharaoh. The glory of all that God had in store for Joseph remained true not only after the Pharaoh appointed him to oversee the land but also and especially as he spent years slaving away and many more years waiting with a patient hope in prison.

So how can we learn to live, love, and patiently wait like Joseph? How can we patiently trust that through our messy, chaotic, and imperfect motherhood, we are responding to the great call to "go therefore and make disciples of all nations" (Matthew 28:19) within our own homes? Well, sweet mommas, maybe one who has toiled through her motherhood and learned that the life-giving fruit of a patient hope can speak the words we need. Mother of ten and grandmother to many, Alicia Hernon gently speaks of slowing the demands of progress. With a deep love for her Heavenly Father and a passion for encouraging parents, Alicia counsels the young mom's heart to let go of all that is not yet perfected and to instead trust that God is at work and growing roots within the patient waiting. I pray that her words will encourage the weary heart and remind each mother of the profound gift of her life, the life she generously gives away for the glory of God's kingdom.

Love Is Patient

ALICIA HERNON

Dear Younger Mom,

I know you are so excited and ready to jump into family life. You want to be an amazing, dedicated, fantastic mom! But how? Well, girl, the first thing you need to do is to learn how to love. But the trick is, it is going to take you a *lifetime*.

The obvious love you need to learn is the love of your husband and children. That is challenging, but most ladies realize that comes with the territory. You also need to learn to love God. Through this vocation, you will learn how to respond with love to him. But finally, and probably the most difficult, is to love yourself. Ah! This is what you didn't expect and find the most challenging love of all.

There will be times now and in the next few years when you think, "I used to be a good person before I had kids!" You will find yourself saying the meanest things you have ever said to anyone in your life, and you will be barking them at a four-year-old child! How discouraging! Long gone are the days when you felt in control, emotionally even, and peaceful on a daily basis. I know you feel frustrations that you didn't expect with this job of being a mom, but there is no other way to grow other than going through these tough, difficult times. Be patient with your growth. The growth will come!

The days with babies and toddlers seem long. I know you feel like you are doing the same things over and over again, like a squirrel in a wheel—working so hard but getting nowhere. You clean up the same toys over and over. You make the same meals and wash the same clothes. Progress in holiness and growth in character seems to be nonexistent.

But deep within you, something is happening. Roots are growing. Roots of dependence on God, shedding of your pride and self-sufficiency, roots that are reaching for the water of life that is the life of God himself. It is when you are dry and needy that those roots will grow deep searching for God, searching for his living water. You will find that water! As a result, the roots that have grown will stabilize you in the years to come. The growth of roots takes a long time, and it is a growth that is mostly unseen, but it is still happening!

There will be a day when you find yourself exhausted and worn out by caring for the children, growing a new baby inside you, and working in the home. You will feel like you can't do it anymore. You will feel like a failure. On that day, go to Jesus! Run to him in the Blessed Sacrament and throw yourself on his mercy! When this happens, you will experience the depth of his love. You will know that you are SEEN and KNOWN and LOVED. I know how badly you want to be perfect and to do everything the "right" way, but that standard that you use to measure your holiness is not the standard that Our Lord uses. He is so much kinder, gentler, and more patient than we are. Learn from him how to love others, but more importantly, learn from him how to love YOURSELF.

> Be patient. You can't see it from the outside, but the struggles you experience along with the frustrations are changing you on the inside.

Be patient. You can't see it from the outside, but the struggles you experience along with the frustrations are changing you on the inside. The more aware you are of your own sinfulness, the more aware you can be of his mercy. It feels like you are less holy, but the reality is that there is no going backward. You will never be the girl you were before. You are now growing into a woman. Don't look at your life in terms of how you have grown in the past year; look at how you have grown these past five or even ten years!

I hear you lamenting over your struggles with the toddlers. You expect so much of yourself and of them! It's ok—you don't have to have it all figured out tomorrow, or the next day, or the next year! Twenty-five years later I can tell you: the learning never ends! The difference between me and you is that you think you need to have it figured out right now. You think there is a secret recipe or a method or a quick trick that will give you the results you desire. My dear, stop looking for those things! Yes, it is wise to seek wisdom from others and learn from those who have gone before you, but there are some lessons that are difficult (or maybe even impossible?) to learn intellectually. You have to experience them. That is why you need to be patient with yourself and recognize that you don't have to get an "A" in mothering right now. (Here's a secret—even those moms you admire, who seem like they have it all together, don't feel like they are succeeding all the time either!) The secret recipe that these ladies have found is to approach your mothering with eyes wide open, ready to learn from your failures, your struggles, and the children themselves. This is what I have learned over the years—that learning to be the mom you are called to be is a lifetime endeavor, so be patient as you learn.

Be patient with the kids too. If they aren't sharing, keep teaching them to share, and be patient with them. If they haven't learned how to read yet, that's OK. Give it time. If they don't seem as advanced as other little kids, it's OK. Give it time. Your job is to be present. That's what those kids need.

Don't push them to grow up!
Enjoy their laughter, silliness,
and childlike hearts.
They will change as they grow.

Instead of spending your emotional energy on worry, slow down! Take the time to look at the little ones where they are and who they are. Don't push them to grow up! Enjoy their laughter, silliness, and childlike hearts. They will change as they grow.

Looking back, you will wish you had spent more time watching the kids play, gazing at your babies, and not demanding so much of the big kids. They have their own journey to travel, and just as God is taking care of you, he is going to take care of them, too. It doesn't all depend on you. What does God want from you? He wants you to be present because that is where he is. Not in the worries for their future, not in the regrets of the past, but right here, right now.

Your husband. Ah, yes! That man you adore who you have pledged your life to and who is your path to holiness. Be patient with him, too! I know right now you want him to be able to read your mind—to know what you need when you need it. Guess what? That will happen over time! He will get better and better at knowing you, your needs, and your desires. But he will not know how to do this unless you are patient with him and teach him. This will require vulnerability on your part. You will have to open yourself to him and reveal your desires, taking the risk that he may not respond the way you want him to. Be patient. He loves you and wants the best for you. He needs time, just as you do, to learn how to love you.

I know you want him to be perfect right now. Immediately. Oh well! Just as you cannot force growth in your children or in yourself, you cannot force it in him either. Just know that it will come over time. He is a great man, a holy man, who wants God and your best just as you want his best. Keep encouraging him and enabling him to find the time to pray that he needs and the mentors and friends that he needs, and give him your admiration and respect. Keep in your mind a vision of the man you know he can be and the man he is. When you show your deep admiration for him, you give him the fuel he needs to continue his growth. A man wants most to be admired by the woman he loves, and your husband loves and prizes you above all others. He is called by God to love you and lay down his life

for you. You are called by God to respect him and hold him in high esteem, allowing him to protect and shelter you. Trust that God is working in your husband and you honor him when you allow him to care for you. He will not care for you perfectly all the time—that is for sure! But that is where the patience comes in. Give him time for growth.

Through the years, you will have the great privilege of watching your darling boys become men, and your precious girls, your "beautiful dolls," become women and then mothers themselves. There is no greater privilege in life than raising a human person to know, love, and serve God. Praise him every day for his goodness to you and for calling you to this mighty work. Always remember that the work is his alone. Just as the growth of the children within your womb was a complete gift of God that you simply cooperated with, so too the growth of these children from childhood to adulthood is a process that you will also beautifully cooperate in, but not control. Your job is to nurture the process and provide the raw materials for healthy growth.
Be patient with this work in your children, your husband, and in you. These lessons of love will take a lifetime to learn.

You got this girl!
Love,
FUTURE YOU

- PRAYER -

*Lord, I praise and thank you for loving me
with an unwavering and immovable love.
You call me your beloved,
regardless of how slowly I have grown
in virtue, trust, surrender, and love.
Please give me the heart to love my children
with the same kind of patient love.
And when the enemy robs me
from seeing the beauty that is set out before me,
so that the only thing I can see is what is not yet;
not yet grown, not yet accomplished, not yet healed,
not yet virtuous, please cleanse my eyes
with your love and restore my vision
to a patient trust.
Jesus came to "give sight to the blind,"
so I will delight in being able to see the mission
of my motherhood clearly once again.*

Amen.

Love Is Kind

Be the living expression of God's kindness; kindness in your face, kindness in your eyes, kindness in your smile.

ST. TERESA OF CALCUTTA

Why is it that our children have their greatest meltdowns, fights, and tear-filled sessions with their siblings and parents, while we mothers most easily use harsh words, or quite frankly show the ugliest side of ourselves to these people we love the most, those precious ones within our own homes? Maybe, it is because our tolerance and mercy toward each other's shortcomings grow thin over time. Or perhaps, we simply feel safe enough to show our whole selves, warts and all, to the people we are confident love us the most. Maybe, deep down we securely know that they won't abandon us because a door was slammed, an eye was rolled, or a voice was raised. Yet, St. Teresa of Calcutta speaks to this tragedy when she says, "It is easy to love the people far away. It is not always easy to love those close to us. It is easier to give a cup of rice to relieve hunger than to relieve the loneliness and pain of someone unloved in our own home."[4]

Kindness is one of those traits we often overlook as an obvious, yet trivial, virtue we try to instill in our rambunctious two-year-olds who have yet to learn the importance of sharing. "Be Kind," we frequently say and often use as the main mantra in important anti-bullying campaigns. Yet, kindness should not merely be a behavioral tactic used to help toddlers behave or to rid schools of oppressive actions. Kindness is a vitally important facet of love that should be nurtured and strengthened within the walls of our home between those who share flesh and blood. In fact, the etymology of the word *kind* is that it comes from the Old English word "cynd," referring to "kin" or family. Family is quite literally at the origin of kindness. Yet, although this ancient root emphasized the concept of kinship, we frequently find it most difficult to consistently practice the virtue of kindness in our motherhood. The kids act out, battle over seemingly small ordeals, break another expensive electronic device, and all too often take our blood, sweat, and tears for granted. We can grow resentful, exhausted, and quite frankly weary. So kindness slowly seeps out the drafty windows of our hearts and homes.

> Yet, God shows us that kindness
> is not trivial or just a mere mantra
> to be echoed, but rather
> a vital part of our humanity,
> especially the humanity in our homes.

Yet God shows us that kindness is not trivial or just a mere mantra to be echoed, but rather a vital part of our humanity, especially the humanity in our homes. The Son of Man personified kindness. Jesus who is "the Way" demonstrates the importance of kindness and compassion through his loving actions. He healed the hemorrhaging, dined with sinners, fed the hungry, defended the children, touched and cured the untouchable, and even forgave those who crucified him. His entire life on earth was one long heroic act of kindness. Jesus shows us that kindness is far greater than socially acceptable politeness or courtesy. It is the vital "quality of being generous, helpful, and caring about other people."[5]

But the Son of Man didn't come to merely just show us kindness. Rather, God calls us, as newly adopted sons and daughters of God, to *be kind*. Through St. Paul, God commands kindness as a rule to living out our new lives in Christ, "Be kind to one another, tenderhearted, forgiving one another, as God in Christ forgave you" (Ephesians 4:32). So too, the *Catechism of the Catholic Church* emphasizes the need for this kindness:

> The free gift of adoption requires on our part continual conversion and *new life*. Praying to our Father should develop in us ... *the desire to become like him*: though created in his image, we are restored to his likeness by grace; and must respond to this grace. We must remember ... and know that when we call God "our Father" we ought to behave as sons of God. You cannot call the God of all *kindness* your Father if you preserve a cruel and inhuman heart; for in this case you no longer have in you the marks of the heavenly Father's *kindness*. We must contemplate the beauty of the Father without ceasing and adorn our souls accordingly. (CCC 2784, emphasis added)

So how do we adorn our souls with the kindness of our Heavenly Father? When the days of chaos and messes overwhelm our maternal minds, how can we stay steadfast on the course of love and compassion? Perhaps the heart of a mother who has unmasked the world's counterfeits to kindness can provide the tender encouragement we need to reflect Christ's kindness back onto the little souls in our home. Heidi Bratton, beautiful momma of six, has a deep passion for strengthening the domestic church. I pray her heart and her words will help us remain faithful to living out our motherhood with a love and kindness that ripples through the generations to come. In the words of Abraham Lincoln, "Kindness is the only service that will stand the storm of life and not wash out. It will wear well and will be remembered long after the prism of politeness or the complexion of courtesy has faded away."

Love Is Kind

HEIDI BRATTON

Hello, Darling Younger Self,

I know you're a bit overwhelmed with caring for your newborn at the same time that your firstborn is heading off to college. That whole bundle of feelings and fears you are having right now? Laughing and sobbing in the same minute? Totally normal. But I have incredibly good news. You are going to adore bringing this new little guy to visit his older siblings at college. Hang in there! The up-and-coming season of motherhood will be one of your all-time favorites, I promise.

As I peer into the rearview mirror, however, and look tenderly at you following the birth of your sixth-born, my heart wilts for you, just a little bit.

You, my darling, are working so hard to love and care for everyone around you. You are not getting much slack, you have very little help, and sleep deprivation is wearing you paper thin. At your core, you are nothing if not a go-getter! You are a truth-seeker, and you have never shied away from doing difficult things. Every day you actively welcome the working of the Holy Spirit in your life, both personally and professionally, and I dearly love all these parts of you.

But, sweet one, as admirable as all these qualities are, all the "work" you do with them will not "work" in the way you think it should. The willingness to do hard things for the sake of love will not, by itself, "work" to bring lasting joy and peace to you, nor to the husband and children you love more than your own life. Neither are these qualities, alone, going to guarantee the harvest of love that you so ardently desire; a harvest where all your loved ones know, love, and serve him who is Love. I am sorry. The adage you were taught in childhood, "God helps those who help themselves," is quite wrong.

Knowing you as I do, I get that this is not welcome news. So, before I go any further, I want you to know that you can take a break from reading this letter anytime you want. Getting acquainted with the biblical and sacramental Jesus and becoming that "best version of yourself" that everyone is always talking about, is going to take longer and be a far more humbling endeavor than you are currently imagining.

So, go. Take a long, hard run if you need to. Bake something delicious, listen to music on repeat, or go on a micro-adventure with the kids to quench that little flame of anger that ignited at the mere suggestion that all the hard work you have done, are doing, and will do for the sake of loving others well, will never be enough on its own. I know, it feels insulting, especially when it also feels like few others are willing to do hard things to love you well. Oh, darling, that one hit the mark, didn't it? I am so sorry. It's okay to let the tears well up. Let them roll down your cheeks. Give them time. When you are ready, will you, please, let my wilted heart pour a little hope on your enflamed heart?

Here's the first thing I wish you could know more deeply right now: you are not on your own. I know it feels that way, and you're not going to get out of doing hard things, but continuing to think that everything is all up to you is not helping and may instead harden your heart.

Would you be willing to consider just two verses from Scripture about work that are actually true?

"Whatever your task, work heartily, as serving the Lord and not men" (Colossians 3:23).

"But seek first his kingdom and his righteousness, and all these things shall be yours as well" (Matthew 6:33).

Maybe let's take that pause with these Scriptures. Right here. Right now.

Breathe.
Pray.

And take some time to wonder at how much softer and kinder these verses are than that old adage.

The willingness to do hard things for the sake of love will not, by itself, "work" to bring lasting joy and peace to you, nor to the husband and children you love more than your own life.

Beautiful. Are you ready to connect again?

See, sweet momma, charging ahead and doing hard things on your own, even with good intentions, will lead you to a state of exhaustion and frustration, and I don't want that for you. A second idea, a secret sauce if you will, that I want to share with you about avoiding that unpleasant state of fatigue is just this: while you are doing hard things with the Lord's help, you also need to be kind with others and with yourself.

The mothering work of shepherding little souls toward heaven is not another accomplishment to be checked off. The real-life "work" of shepherding souls requires a higher tolerance for trial and error, a softer touch, and more imagination than you usually think it should. Little souls (and big) are precious, but also rowdy, opinionated, and arrive in your arms with presets that you are not going to be able to erase. Remember how you could not find one potty training program that worked for all the kids? And so you "gave up" and started rewarding even near misses with gumballs and M&Ms for some of the kids, and shockingly, it worked? That wasn't giving up. That was pouring on the secret sauce, baby! Loving kindness-in-action to the toddlers and to yourself.

Even as I chuckle with the memories of all the toddlers eventually showing off their new underwear to every friend and stranger who walked in the house, I also understand that the non-programmable aspects of mothering discourage you. Allow me to turn your gaze back to the idea that shepherding little souls is a

process, and as tenderly as I can, suggest that it's your go-getter prioritization of efficiency and end results that often causes you so much discouragement. I can see why you take that approach, really, I can. Right now your plate is piled so high with things to do that it really looks like you've got an active Hawaiian volcano on that plate! Could it be possible, however, that you think that being tender and kind while clearing that plate is some sort of extra luxury, a nice bonus *if* you have the time and energy for it? Have you, maybe, been stretched so thin for so long that you feel you are stuck in the position of choosing either efficiency or kindness just to get through the day?

Oh, my goodness, dear one, I hit the mark again, didn't I? This time I can almost see you squinting your eyes at me and huffing, "Really? Let me get this straight, you want me to just sugarcoat hard things with kindness and not worry about the results? Yeah, sure. How is that supposed to work, exactly?" Well, I am glad you asked, because right now is the perfect time for you to not put up your dukes, and instead of trying harder to understand, try more kindly.

Pause.
Breathe.
Pray.

And wonder at these new ideas that mothering is more like embracing a disorderly process than designing a perfect program, and that sweetening the process with kindness is fundamental, not a froufrou extra …

Hello again, darling, and welcome back! I know you are going to love the third idea I want to share with you because it is super practical. A significant part of why you have not yet figured out the importance of flavoring the work of mothering with loving kindness is that counterfeits abound! Would you read the following verse and consider it?

"Do you not know that a little *leaven* leavens all the dough? Cleanse out the old leaven that you may be new dough, as you really are unleavened. For Christ, our Paschal Lamb, has been sacrificed. Let us, therefore, celebrate the festival, not with the old *leaven*, the *leaven* of malice and evil, but with the unleavened bread of sincerity and truth" (1 Corinthians 5:6–8, emphasis added).

Unfortunately, darling girl, parts of you were formed in the ways of counterfeit kindness, and these ways, like leaven, got added into the "bread" of your life. These counterfeits are malicious and evil because they distort the meaning of loving kindness for you. For years now, you have been trying to "punch down" counterfeit kindnesses, as if they were ballooning lumps of yeast dough. It would be an incredible liberation for you to see these counterfeit kindnesses for the inflated lies that they truly are, so here are just a few for you to look at:

1. Saccharine flattery, which is meant to emotionally manipulate rather than express love.
2. Trying to rewrite experiences of pain with spiritual Pollyannaisms instead of validating the pain.
3. The elevation of polite tolerance over open honesty.
4. Insincere applause.
5. "Random acts of kindness" being extolled as if they were a sort of magical pixie-dust.
6. People-pleasing.
7. Giving too much and with strings attached.

Open your eyes, my lovely younger self, and strive not to be duped any longer by these counterfeits when others try to add them to your "bread" or your life. Strive even harder to see when you, yourself, try to introduce them into relationships.

Instead, pause.
Breathe.
Pray.

Pause.
Breathe.
Pray.

And wonder how you might practice the following authentically scriptural expressions of loving kindness instead:

1. Noticing and quietly praising what is truly excellent.
2. Not needing everything to always be okay. Bringing your pain to the Lord, just sitting with him and letting him love. Sitting and praying silently with others in their pain instead of rushing to minimize, solve, or resolve it.
3. Being courageously and meekly honest, even when you know it will probably call fire down on your head.
4. Being on the lookout for and specifically applauding whatsoever things are true, good, and beautiful.
5. Offering intentionally thought-out acts of timely, fitting kindness to specific individuals, most of whom are not random strangers.
6. Respecting your personal gifts and limits and letting your prayerful "yes" be "yes" and your prayerful "no" be "no."
7. Giving freely what you can from what you have been given.

This has been a lot to digest, hasn't it? Thank you, darling, for sticking with me. The last, mind-blowingly beautiful thing

I would love for you to consider is just this: all trustworthy, loving kindness is an imitation of God's loving kindness, a tender, merciful kindness that is not results-oriented. Do you remember the second Scripture reading chosen for your wedding? It was 1 John 4:19: "We love, because he first loved us." Go back and replace the word "love" with the word "kind," and the verse becomes a sweet summary of all I hope you might know sooner rather than later: You are not on your own. You can shepherd your little ones with more loving kindness, because he first shepherded you with loving kindness. Shepherding with this approach will not hinder your work but elevate it to an authentic imitation of the Lord's shepherding of you.

So, what do you think? Are you up for a mindset shift? The Lord is an inexhaustible wellspring of all you need, and trust me, that mountainous plate of hot lava you've got there is not going dormant anytime soon, so aligning your heart more and more with his heart is your million-dollar mom move! I hope you'll give it a shot, and I'll look forward to meeting that even more beautiful, best version of you! His grace *will* be enough for you and for everyone you love. In the meantime, don't forget to pause, breathe, pray, and wonder at the work of art God is going to make of that overflowing plate of hot lava, in his time. It won't be perfect, but it will be beautiful, I promise!

Oh, and crank more music while you are cooking dinner.

I love you so,

YOUR MORE SEASONED SELF

- PRAYER -

*Dear Jesus, thank you for showering me
with your endless kindness. You are a generous and good God
who never withholds your kindness
even when, by the world's standard, I may not deserve it.
Please give me the grace to allow that same kindness
to overflow from within and pour out
upon those within my home.
I desire to be a tender and kind
maternal instrument of your love.
But I am often overwhelmed with the demands of daily life.
So, when life gets chaotic and my heart gets distracted
with all of the to-dos I have yet to accomplish,
please, Lord, help me to pause, breathe, and pray.
Allow me to remember that your calling
to me is less about what I do and
more about how I do things
to make my heart more like your heart.*

Amen.

Love Does Not Envy

If all flowers wanted to be roses, nature would lose her springtime beauty, and the fields would no longer be decked out with little wild flowers.

ST. THÉRÈSE OF LISIEUX

We were having a lively dinner table discussion about the Ten Commandments. My daughter was preparing for her First Reconciliation, and her gang of siblings decided to make a game out of recalling the commandments she was memorizing. As we neared the end of the list, I was suddenly overwhelmed with a truth that was very clear but that somehow had never hit me all these years: The commands that "You shall not covet your neighbor's wife … or anything that belongs to your neighbor" do not merely forbid *taking* another's spouse or possessions. No, my friends, "You shall not commit adultery" and "You shall not steal" are already two of the Ten Commandments. Instead, the word "covet," meaning to unjustly desire what another has, or in simpler terms, "envy," is underlined by the King of the Heavens as a sin.

"Envy is a capital sin. It refers to the sadness at the sight of another's goods and the immoderate desire to acquire them for oneself, even unjustly" (CCC 2539). Usually concealed, it operates unlike most sins. When we use God's name in vain, skip Mass, lie, gossip, or steal a cookie from the cookie jar, others frequently take notice. However, the very private emotion of coveting what another has is often hidden not only from others but even and most destructively from ourselves. So God, in his perfect fatherly protection and unceasing love, *commands* that we do not fall prey to the sin that brought death into the world and nailed his Son to the Cross (see Wisdom 2:23 and Matthew 27:18).

> **However, the very private emotion of coveting what another has is often hidden not only from others but even and most destructively from ourselves.**

I was in awe; how could I have breezed over these two commands with such carelessness all these years? Envy is not a sin we like to admit, even to ourselves. We frequently view envy as part of the dirty antics of jealous teens and adolescents or materialistic

lovers of the world. Yet, we mommas are far from exempt from this great command. And when we do admit to envy, we usually downplay it as a silly little emotion. But St. Cyprian warns us of the gravity of this sin: "To be jealous of the good that you see and to be envious of those better than one's self seems in the eyes of some to be a slight and moderate wrong, most beloved brothers, and when it is thought to be light and moderate, it is not feared; when it is not feared, it is contemned; when it is contemned, it is not easily avoided; and it becomes a dark and hidden *source of destruction*, which, when it is not perceived so that it can be avoided by the provident, secretly afflicts improvident minds."[6]

Envy is one of the most dangerous afflictions in our motherhood. "Why don't my children listen to me like hers do?", "Her house is never messy", "Ugh her meals are always homemade and fresh", "Her husband is constantly helping her with the kids, but mine is always gone," or "They are always so put together for Mass, while we look like we just climbed our way out of the woods" are just a few of the heart cries that are being whispered from the depths of mothers' souls across the globe.

We may even begin by praising and encouraging other mothers. But once our own innate goodness and value feel threatened by

the goodness in another, we, like Saul with David, may begin to foster a sharp jealousy and disdain for them. In the beginning, King Saul loved David greatly, even desiring his companionship (see Samuel 16:21). When the time came for David to enter battle with the giant Goliath, Saul, himself, clothed the poor shepherd boy in his own armor and sword. David was too small to wear Saul's gear, but he won the impossible win, with nothing more than a sling and stone. Excited by the victory, King Saul even set David over his army (see 1 Samuel 18:5). But once he heard the women singing, "Saul has slain his thousands, and David his ten thousands" (1 Samuel 18:7), Saul's once great love and admiration turned into envy and hatred, an angry envy that would threaten his own life until the day he eventually took it.

Our own envy can similarly lead to our own self-imposed deaths: death of relationships, death of love in our motherhood, and death of our trust in God. Even when no one else notices, envy poisons our souls, suffocates our hearts, and rots our bones (see Proverbs 14:30). It is not only toxic for our own bodies and souls, but it villainizes those we envy within the depths of our very beings. It entangles itself within sisterly friendships, and if left unchecked, the sharp blades of envy will sever these once life-giving relationships altogether. When we secretly wish our kids were as smart, holy, or well-behaved as hers seem, or that our family was as large, as Instagram-worthy, or as globe-trotting as hers, we rob ourselves of the grace of gratitude. When we live with this scarcity mindset, we become blind to the abundance of God in our lives. Our envy leads to a poisonous discontent for all that God has given us and breathes a subtle "we aren't good enough" or even "*you* aren't good enough" message to the people in our homes. And this, my friends, is not only like drinking poison ourselves but as if we are slowly mixing it within each cup of love we try to serve our children.

**Every single mother,
in her unqiue loveliness,
was carefully crafted by God.**

Every single mother, in her unique loveliness, was carefully crafted by God. He knows what will draw us individually and more perfectly into communion with him, a communion that is the greatest human experience on this side of heaven's veil. The unique gifts and crosses, triumphs and defeats, and joys and sorrows are designed, if we allow them, to draw not only our hearts but those around us, especially our children, to God and his perfect love. When our story was meant for us, and us alone, what have we to be jealous of?

But when the crushing blows of life fall on us, we can lose sight of our loving and active God. Our eyes turn down, we fret, we worry, and we *compare*. So when we find ourselves swallowed by a debilitating envy that feeds the lie that everyone else's lives are perfect and well-orchestrated, how do we pick ourselves up from the depths of despair to pursue goodness and beauty in our motherhood once again? How do we climb out from under the sheets of shame and envy? Maybe a mother who once found herself with hot and heavy tears full of fear and unworthiness can show us what it means to let go of envy and to live our motherhood with the Grace of acceptance.

A spiritual director with a deep love for God and a passion for encouraging women, Heather Voccola has journeyed through some of the roughest terrains. Abandoned by her husband, this single mother of two learned what it means to strip herself of shame and envy and instead welcome the story God wanted to tell through her. I pray that her words become a source of encouragement that will help heal us from the blinding destruction of coveting what our neighbor has and open our eyes to see the peace and freedom that comes when we accept and trust "that in *everything* God works for good with those who love him" (Romans 8:28, emphasis added).

Love Does Not Envy

HEATHER VOCCOLA

Dear Sweet Mama,

I want you to know that I see you.

I see you buried under this mountain of shame, trying to keep everything together for your amazing and beautiful girls. I see you trying your best to make it all work—to make ends meet, spend time with the girls, and work on your prayer life. I know there are not enough hours in the day for you to get everything done by yourself, so it is okay if the floor isn't mopped or the laundry isn't folded. You aren't neglecting these things on purpose—it doesn't make you a bad mother. I see that it is sometimes difficult for you to sit still in Adoration right now, but I want you to know that even if you need to be pacing in the back because of your nervous energy and anxiety, Jesus loves you, and it is good that you came to see him. He sees your pain and your shame even more clearly than I do, and he came to redeem you from all of it.

Even now, after all these years, I remember that pain and shame—not understanding how divorce would fit into God's plan for your family. How could this happen to your

two beautiful, amazing, and faithful daughters? How could this happen to you after you did all you could to put your marriage first and challenge your spouse to grow into the husband and father God created him to be? Why would God allow this great suffering?

I know your mother's heart is breaking with the grief of not wanting life to be this way. I know that you look around at all your Catholic friends and what you perceive to be their perfect Catholic marriages and wonder why it's different for them. Why are they okay when you are not? Why did their husbands follow after their conversions and yours did not? Why did theirs stay and yours did not? Comparing yourself to them will only make you crazy. God will give you all you need. Remember that his plan for them is for their good, just as yours is for you. I know it doesn't make it hurt less or make the longing to have that same security go away, but you will find peace in it.

I know too that sometimes, in the very dark of night, when it looks like this pain will last forever and you have no more tears left to cry, you want only failure and difficulties for the man who walked out on you. You don't want him to be happy because it comes at the expense of you and your girls' suffering. I know it feels like the hurt and anger are just too much in these moments. But I want you to remember that real love does not want that. Jesus calls you to something more. Real love wants the best of God's plan for everyone—even those who hurt us the most.

You don't want bitterness to define you. It takes energy you don't have to continue to hold onto bitterness and pain. So even though

I know it feels like the hurt and anger are just too much in these moments. But I want you to remember that real love does not want that. Jesus calls you to something more.

your heart is truly breaking for what the future will hold now for you and your girls, I promise that it won't always be like this. I know because I have lived it. You can trust me. Forgiving is an act of the will; feeling something or nothing at all doesn't impact your choice to forgive. And you can do it over and over again through the years as the circumstances change. This is real love. This is what Jesus calls you to. This is what he asks you to model for your girls.

Do you remember that Saturday morning, the first one when the girls had slept over with their dad? That was the morning you didn't get out of bed. Everything hurt, like the pain in your heart had taken over your whole body. You lay there just watching the red numbers on the digital clock ticking the time away, willing it to be Sunday night when the girls would return. I remember how you kept thinking to yourself, "I don't have to relive this minute of time ever again." And you would have stayed in that bed all weekend, if not for something a friend gave you. It was something simple, but it would change your life forever.

It was a statue of Our Lady.

That afternoon, you set the figure of Mary in the center of the table but facing out the window as if that would keep Mary from seeing you in your disarray. Do you remember standing with the statue looking out the window? It was sunny outside, even though it was one of the darkest days in your heart. It was Saturday, the day for family time.

Everyone you knew was living out a normal weekend of balancing kids' activities with chores and date night, but your family was shattered. Remembering those hectic and crazy family days would now become a cross for you. It's hard to know that you can no longer have what everyone around you seems to take for granted, but I promise you and the girls will adjust. There is a peace that comes with acceptance; it just takes patience until you get there.

Finally, you knelt before the statue on the hardwood floor and said aloud just one prayer:

Dear Mary, I consecrate to you my girls. There are times when I am no longer able to be there like a mother should. You have to do it. You have to be their mother when I am not able to.

It has been 18 years since you entrusted your girls, your whole mother's heart, really, to the Blessed Virgin. I'm writing to you today, dear Sweet Mama, all these years later, because she heard your prayer, and she brought it before her Son, Jesus. And they answered your prayer by blessing your girls and keeping them safe. Mary also said something else to you that day, in words you could only make out much later: *Do whatever he tells you.*

I want you to know that after the divorce, your struggle with your Catholic friend group wasn't meaningless. When some turned away because they wanted to protect their own children from your world of divorce, new girlfriends, and your daughters' new brother, there was nothing you could have done differently to change that. I know that some of the things that were said to you made you feel even more isolated and alone.

I promise that the Lord will provide some new families for you and your girls—families with younger children who don't yet understand all the ugly details of what life can be like. These folks will welcome you and your daughters at this time of your life.

You don't yet know this, but you were actually blazing a trail for a few other Catholic families you know who ended up in similar circumstances over the years. When you said yes to the Lord's invitation to give talks and write articles about divorce and annulment, this encouragement made a difference in the lives of other women. This is what mothers do. They work to overcome their own suffering so they can be attentive to the needs of others. They do this most specifically for their own children, but real love calls us to do this for everyone.

Do you remember how you sometimes felt completely overwhelmed by life, and everywhere you looked, everyone around you had a partner in the struggle? I know it is hard to make decisions about everything when there isn't someone else on the team. Finances, college, teenagers breaking the rules ... How do you figure all of this out by yourself?

Mary also said something else to you that day, in words you could only make out much later: *Do whatever he tells you.*

Wanting what everyone else has obscures what is actually happening in your own life. I know it is impossible to see right now, but you have a partner too. It is the Lord himself! He is always by your side. He yearns to know all that is going on with you and your girls. Turn to him in prayer and set these things before him. Recognize that he has placed people in your life who care about you and can help you. Remember the encouragement from Mary: *Do whatever he tells you.* The plan he is inviting you to participate in will take you to places and ask you to do things you never thought possible.

I want to tell you how the suffering of your mother's heart will make you attentive and available to other daughters, not just the flesh and blood girls God gave you. These other daughters are young women trying to find their way in the faith, or who are separated from their own mothers through loss or circumstance. They will be able to turn to you for care and counsel, and they will. God is asking you to create a space to receive these women, but not just these young ladies, all women. He is asking you to pick up and go where he sends you. And once your own young ladies are out in the world, living for Jesus, you will.

Everything you are going through in these most dark and difficult moments and all the little swords that pierce your mother's heart, the Lord has allowed. He is asking you to set aside your envy, not to compare but to embrace your own path, and to remember our God is a God of promises. He brings good from all things. Most especially, I want to assure you that as your girls embrace the faith as their own, there will be bumps, but there will be straight paths, too.

Your example of strength and your ability to overcome the bitterness has set them moving in the right direction in all the most important ways. Only God knows whether or not they will follow his path to its end, but you fought valiantly to give them all they deserved and to teach them that Jesus asks more from us. He calls us to real love. Envy has no place in the heart of a Christian.

In Thanksgiving for you,

ELDER DAUGHTER OF THE KING

- PRAYER -

*Lord, thank you for showing me
that your Fatherly heart
desires nothing short of all of me:
the broken, the full, the beautiful, the messy,
the abandoned, the restored.
I pray that when my heart becomes distracted
with what seems to be lacking,
you will give me the grace
to see all that is abundant.
Transform this little and feeble heart
into one that trusts in the bigness
and beauty of your divine plans,
plans for me, my children,
and all those that I encounter.
Give me the strength to surrender the chains
of comparison and allow you to clothe me
with the conviction of your care.*

Amen.

Love Is Not Boastful

You must not be discouraged or let yourself become dejected if your actions have not succeeded as perfectly as you intended. What do you expect? We are made of clay and not every soil yields the fruits expected by the one who tills it. But let us always humble ourselves and acknowledge that **we are nothing if we lack the Divine assistance.**

ST. PADRE PIO

———

"Aw, momma, my ashes disappeared already," my sweet four-year-old said to me an hour after Mass on Ash Wednesday. I could understand her disappointment, for the novelty of wearing ashes all day as a declaration of our love for Jesus feels like an honor and a special duty. But as I walked by our hall mirror, I saw that I too no longer had any remnants of ashes on my forehead. Then I noticed how my own heart sank. And swiftly Jesus' words echoed in my heart. "And when you pray, you must not be like the hypocrites; for they love to stand and pray in the synagogues and at the street corners, that they may be seen by men" (Matthew 6:5). No, as I was always reminded as a little girl, my ashes should not be a tool that the enemy can use to tempt my heart toward a boasting Catholicism. Wear them but for God alone.

Yet, the temptation to fall into subtle gloating does not apply only to this outward sign of our inner declaration. No, for the Enemy, like a trembling and terrified sniper, has his dirty eyes laser-focused on using boasting to attack our magnificent and divinely appointed vocation of motherhood, a vocation we so desperately desire to do well.

We wholeheartedly desire to leave behind a legacy of love for our families. Sometimes we utterly struggle.

We wholeheartedly desire to leave behind a legacy of love for our families. Sometimes we utterly struggle. The house is a mess, the meals are burned, the kids fought, I yelled, and a dark cloud seemed to be hovering over me like something out of a cartoon. Yet, other days we succeed. We hustle along as boo-boos are kissed, backs are scratched, and snuggles are abounding. We operate like air traffic controllers directing schedules to ensure each child is on time for soccer practice, ski coaching, and karate

lessons. Finally, we even successfully corral the troops and land in the captain's bed while little ones wriggle and squirm as we end the day with the daily Gospel and family prayers. *Phew, I did it,* we whisper as we collapse in bed after making it through a long day void of balls dropped or voices raised.

Perhaps, we even find ourselves in a season where we can look back and realize, *Wow, I have barely lost my temper at all these last few months! I've frequented daily Mass with all the children, baked those meals for the new moms, and given the most thoughtful Christmas gifts. The hubby and I have been getting along so well, and I've made sure to give each kid some much-needed dedicated time and attention. I'm killing it!*

Yes, sweet friend, you are! Delight in this goodness. But then that sneaky voice keeps whispering, "Yes, wow, look how amazing *you* are doing. *You* have worked so hard; you are nailing it." This is where the enemy, in his cunning ways, knows precisely how to poison what is good. And if he is really successful, he may even tempt us to subtly gloat about our success during those playdates or momma coffee hours. "*While I was bringing a meal to my neighbor who just had a new baby*, I remembered I left my

house unlocked." or "There was so much traffic this morning *as the kids and I were on our way to daily Mass.*" The devil's deception is to trick our hearts into believing that we are better, more successful, or more holy than others, and even to believe the lie that we are responsible for our success. *I'm so glad I know I should dress modestly, unlike that mother in the church pew next to me.*

Jesus emphasizes this point when he tells the parable of the Pharisee and the tax collector who went into a temple to pray. "The Pharisee stood and prayed thus with himself, 'God, I thank you that I am not like other men, extortioners, unjust, adulterers, or even like this tax collector. I fast twice a week, I give tithes of all that I get.' But the tax collector, standing far off, would not even lift up his eyes to heaven, but beat his breast, saying, 'God, be merciful to me a sinner!'" (Luke 18:11–13). Jesus slays the way of arrogance when he shares that the tax collector, a despised man amongst the Jews, "went down to his house justified rather than the other; for every one who exalts himself will be humbled, but he who humbles himself will be exalted" (Luke 18:14).

The *Catechism of the Catholic Church* boldly states that "boasting or bragging is an offense against truth" (CCC 2814). Regardless of how easy, hard, messy, or beautiful our days of motherhood are, we must remember the truth that "every good endowment and every perfect gift is from above" (James 1:17). God is Lord of our hearts and homes, and he certainly doesn't want us to use his perfect gifts to boast about our own success, or worse yet to look down upon others. Instead, when we deliver those homemade meals, make it to daily Mass, or enjoy a day void of yelling and full of beauty, we must remember to praise God alone for the pure treasure sent from the heavens into the open and awaiting heart of a momma.

Yet still, as we learn to be stretched in humility and put away from us all boasting, it does not mean dismissing or degrading the creation that we are. Instead, it means keeping our eyes gazing at the face of Jesus. As one author has written, real humility is

God is Lord of our hearts and homes, and he certainly doesn't want us to use his perfect gifts to boast about our own success, or worse yet to look down upon others.

"not thinking less of ourselves but thinking of ourselves *less*."[7] Rest assured, our heroic acts of love are not invisible like the ashes that once faded away. Instead, our Father's heart delights to see his daughter give herself away in love.

So as we move through the messy and magnificent days of motherhood, how can we learn to relish God's goodness and avoid boasting of our own success? Perhaps, a momma of two with an intense passion for the vocation of motherhood can shed light on the humbling beauty and calling of a mother's heart. With a love for her Lord, the lovely Dorothy Pilarski is on a mission to revive the vocation of motherhood. I pray that her words will captivate the mom heart, and reignite it on a beautiful, humbling, and glorious mission of leading hearts in and through love.

Love Is Not Boastful

DOROTHY PILARSKI

Dear Precious Mama,

It's not your imagination.

Yes, it's true, God is leading you in this mysterious adventure of being a mother.

Yes, you have seen it yourself, God is here to help in concrete and practical ways. You have sensed his presence more than once. You have seen the supernatural.

Can you boast about the spiritual gifts you've received? No, you can't boast about gifts, but you can acknowledge them, and relish them.

There's no need to run away or be afraid. In fact, you don't want to miss even one second of it. The years go by so quickly; just like those little old ladies at the grocery stores like to say, "They'll be gone before you know it!"

Don't miss the moments, Mama. Stay right here in the thick of it. Pull up your big girl pants and remember:

"You can do this!"
"You've got what it takes!"
"What's more important than this?"
"Who is the best person to raise your child?"

Yes, I know it's painful sometimes. God is pruning you, he's challenging you, he's consoling you, he's stretching you (both literally and figuratively). He's stripping you of the illusion that confused you into thinking you're independent and you don't need him. You need God, now more than ever.

He's demanding that you develop virtues you have never had (and maybe don't want to have LOL). He's brought you joy, wonder, worry, frustration, sleepless nights, mountain-top moments, and bewildering questions that keep popping into your mind. He's asking you to face yourself.

The crucible, the work, the transformative process of becoming a mother is a divine gift that forges the bond between mother and child. I know you want to forge that bond. I see that you cherish it.

Can we boast of the graces we've been given?
No, love doesn't boast. But we can praise our Lord,
for the gift of trusting in him.

My Precious Mama, as you give up parts of yourself out of love for your child, as you stare down what needs to be stared down, you are claiming your birthright of a well-forged supernatural, loving bond with your child. When you do the work, the child knows it. When you run away….

They know that too. It's exhilarating sometimes.

The giggles, the singing, those first steps, the first words uttered, the belly flops, the joys and the ecstasy of knowing you are so needed and oh so loved. Whether it's staring at your baby sleep, experiencing mystical moments nursing in the middle of the night, or dancing delightfully to this song or that—watching your son or daughter get a goal, get accepted into college—all these zillions of moments that bring you to heaven and back are like stars in the sky. You'll look back one day at the galaxy of moments that you, Mama, have helped create.

Can we boast looking back? No, instead we prayerfully remember, *"There but for the grace of God go I."*

Do you have regrets? Hurry up and get to confession. God can redeem every single thing!

Remember, your work as mama is eternally important. God is waiting for your yes. Remember, he waited for the yes of Mother Mary. Cling to your rosary, pray fervently for your little one.

Have you ever considered that, in a sense, you are holding Jesus in your arms? How would you treat Baby Jesus?

Precious Mama, what do you want your children to say about you when they look back at their childhood?

Do you want them to say, "She kept a clean house"? "She was always busy"? "She studied a lot"? "She prayed a lot"?

Whatever you want them to say, start living it. Believe it or not, Mama, your children are watching (and so is your Creator), and they will say *something* someday! Take a few moments to journal and write about the mother that God is calling you to become.

See yourself through the eyes of your child. It is my prayer for you that your children say: **She Loved.**

I often think back to a workshop I attended for parents of young kids. It really struck me when the speaker said, half-jokingly,

"Be careful how you treat your children; they're the ones likely to choose what old folks' home you'll be living in!"

It's confusing sometimes. It's downright hard to know what to do and where to start. I wish I could sit right beside you and say,

"Don't worry, hon, everything is going to be OK! You are doing just fine. Stop scrolling through Instagram—your child is not an accessory to be dressed up and displayed. Your house is not a TV set to be decorated and posted. And you, beloved Mama, are a treasure in God's eyes. Instead of pouring yourself out to strangers on social media, take that time and pour yourself out to him. Pray without ceasing. Invoke the Holy Spirit."

See yourself through the eyes of your child. It is my prayer for you that your children say: She Loved.

Your child needs your maternal love, not likes. Your house needs to be transformed into a spiritually welcoming home that nourishes, not competes. After all, your baby doesn't know whether you rent

or own the house that you're living in. Your baby really doesn't give a hoot about what brand of stroller you own!

And so here you are, again wondering, *God, is there meaning in all of this? Who would have known this was all going to be so hard and wonderful—all at the same time?*

Yes, my beloved, God is here. And he will continue to be there until the end of time, sweetening your sorrows, fortifying your efforts, holding *you*, Precious Mama, in the palm of his hand. Keep close to him. Keep going to Mass, keep praying, keep reaching out to Jesus, and stay immersed in his Word. Turn to Our Blessed Mother. Don't just cling to your rosary, pray it. And yes, relish and trust in the deposit of grace that has been ***given specifically to you, to mother your little ones, in your own particular way.***

You have been chosen. Need supernatural help?

Remember, you are not alone. God loves you. Mama Mary loves you. The saints love you. Yes, even the Holy Souls in Purgatory love you.

I have experienced the miraculous intercession of my heavenly power team, and so will you!

You have a team of prayer warriors that want to intercede for you, to answer your prayers! And yes, they are here amongst the laundry, lollipops, diapers, loads of dirty dishes, unanswered texts, and innumerable tense conversations.

Never stop praying! Keep reaching out. An answered prayer is just around the corner…

You see, dear Mama, you are God's co-creator. He's doing work in you and through you, that well, you cannot boast of, but you can be sure of.

Stay rooted in him. Remember the moments of awe and wonder as you sensed that your little one was being formed in your womb? On the deepest level, you understood clearly and succinctly the reality of Our Blessed Mother's words, *Let it be done unto me* (see Luke 1:38).

Could you boast about your little one? The perfect little hands, feet, and their delightful eyes, their life are all a gift.

You worked so hard during your pregnancy, eating the right foods, going for medical checkups, swimming, going for long walks, talks, journaling, reading the right books, praying, sitting

**You see, dear Mama,
You are God's co-creator.
He's doing work in you and through you,
that well, you cannot boast of,
but you can be sure of.**

for hours in Eucharistic Adoration, talking endlessly to your girlfriends and yes listening to the musings of your own heart and the heart of your own mother—as God was miraculously and mysteriously doing his work for you.

And so here you are.

Could you boast about the goodness that surrounds you? The remarkable medical care? The available resources? The spiritual direction? Your health? Your doting mom? Your patient husband? The hours in Eucharistic Adoration?

No, you cannot boast of all the blessings, all the gifts that have been showered upon you. Take time now to reflect on them, maybe take a few minutes to journal, and give thanks for them.

God has **entrusted you** with this precious little one. He has great plans for you and your baby. It's bewildering to think that **God has given you the responsibility of teaching your baby about God himself**. He calls you to teach your little one about Jesus, Mother Mary, the saints, and his Catholic Church.

What an awesome and overwhelming responsibility! What a gift to know that God has called you and you need him! You have been chosen for a remarkable mission.

Are you noticing that God is always sending you what you need? Sometimes it's a Bible verse, sometimes it's a home-cooked meal, other times it's a Mother's Helper or a good night's sleep!

"But seek first his kingdom and his righteousness, and all these things shall be yours as well" (Matthew 6:33).

Can you boast in his provision? No, it is all a gift. You can fully rely on providence, it's true. Learning to live with that conviction and trust takes time.

One thing I can promise you, Precious Mama, is this: everything you need can be found in the Eucharist—everything! Receive Jesus worthily and often (daily if you can), going to the Sacrament of Reconciliation. Remember his words: "For my flesh is food indeed, and my blood is drink indeed" (John 6:55).

From time to time, thinking back on your professional accomplishments, perhaps you miss the adrenaline rush of working side by side with like-minded colleagues, perusing trade journals (or writing for them). Perhaps you miss sitting in a civilized, predictable office environment where everything is so pretty, organized, controlled, and sometimes a bit sterile. You are left wondering … *Do I miss being smack in the middle of downtown, grabbing a latte, jumping into a taxi, and getting acknowledgment for my business acumen? Do I miss going to stimulating conferences or fun networking events?*

As you stare out the window, deciding on your next best step, don't torture yourself; that's not what friends do. Instead, pray, seek spiritual direction, and pray some more.

Whether you work full-time, from home, part-time, or are fully trusting in his provision, you are your child's mother, irreplaceable and uniquely their own mother.

I can promise you this, my precious Mama (I'd shout it from the rooftops if I could): if you organize your day so you go to daily Mass, with Jesus at the center of your day, *everything, and I mean everything*, will be given to you, plus some.

LOVE IS NOT BOASTFUL | 85

Can I boast of these life hacks? Daily Mass? Praying the Rosary? Going to confession? Spiritual Direction?
No, they are all divine gifts. If you respond to these lights, my love, it's all grace upon grace.

I have to admit, I sometimes wonder why I am not like other women, who don't seem to need to rest at his feet daily going to Mass. Then God leads me to the words of a saint that encourages me on my path.

"Hear Mass daily; it will prosper the whole day. All your duties will

be performed the better for it and your soul will be stronger to bear its daily cross.
–St. Peter Julian Eymard

Other times, I am tempted to think that in making the decisions I have, like prioritizing raising my children and going to daily Mass, I may somehow be missing out professionally, not keeping up with my contemporaries. But do you know what? As time has passed, the opposite has proved to be true. Again, in my spiritual reading, I will stumble upon the words of a saint that give me the courage to keep following the prompts of the Holy Spirit.

"We need never fear that Mass hinders us in the fulfillment of our temporal affairs; it is altogether the other way around. We may be sure that all will go better and even our business will succeed better than if we have the misfortune not to assist at Mass.
–St. John Vianney

From the bottom of my heart, I pray that you are reassured and inspired to continue following the promptings of Our Blessed Mother, to remain alert to signs and commands of the Holy Spirit, and to remain rooted in the Word of God and writings of our precious Catholic saints.

Love,
YOUR OLDER, WISER SELF

- PRAYER -

*Dear God, thank you for always delighting in me,
for no other reason than for simply being yours.
With a Father's heart,
you have never stopped delighting in me,
just as you ceaselessly delight
in all of your precious creations,
especially the little souls in my home.
Please help rid me of the temptation to brag, boast,
or flaunt the gifts you have lavished upon me.
When the world places a high value
on all that I accomplish,
please give me the grace of humility
and the heart to remember that without you
I can do nothing. It is only in abiding in you
that this heart beats, these lungs breathe,
and this soul loves.
I love you and I thank you.*

Amen.

Love Is Not Proud

The rivers of Grace cannot flow uphill,
up the steep cliff of the proud man's heart.

ST. BERNARD OF CLAIRVAUX

Meal prep, spilled messes, bills to pay, and laundry, oh the never-ending laundry. Since I can remember, my days have been consumed with an endless list of duties to be completed. Motherhood not only hands us a massive pile of to-dos that need tending, but it also gives us the greater honor and responsibility of tending to little hearts. We desire to care well, love well, and *mother* well. So we strategize, read the books, listen to the experts, come up with a plan, and off we race. We make promises to ourselves about the patterns we won't repeat, the things we will complete, and the ways in which we will be good Christian mothers.

We have been tricked into believing that the ultimate motherhood prize is to wear the elusive badge of honor that declares "Super Mom!" My bread is homemade, my kids are well-behaved, and I volunteer to serve at school, church, and the local soup kitchen! We want to show our children, our spouses, our parents, and our peers that we are doing well at this thing called motherhood. All the while our exhausted bodies and spirits continue to cry out: "Am *I* doing enough? How do *I* stack up?"

Rushed, hasty, and frequently short-tempered, we race to get it all done, imploding shrapnel from our inner turmoil onto the ones we set out to love well! Suffocating the good and pure desire to mother well, is a one-letter word that frequently gets in the way. The small and unassuming letter "*I*" pulls our attention off of God and places it squarely on ourselves. Busily focused

With busy eyes set upon ourselves and our performance, we miss gazing into the tiny ones that are looking up at ours.

on ourselves and our performance, we miss gazing into the tiny eyes that are looking up at ours.

Well-intentioned mothers across the world fall into the very trap that stole paradise from our first parents—pride. How our motherhood appears to the world may be as "pleasing to the eye" as the apple was to Adam and Eve. When we focus on our performance our hearts move inward and backward rather than upward and outward. A wave of destruction is left in its wake, and like Adam and Eve, we remain naked and afraid of all that is forward.

"Haughty eyes and a proud heart, the lamp of the wicked, are sin" (Proverbs 21:4). Our secret pride in motherhood has the danger of slowly filling our minds with ourselves, leaving little space for the light of God; a light so bright that it burns out the fields of our ego. A heart moved by a hidden self-conceit will participate in turmoil, sin, and destruction. But this is not and never was God's plan for us. He wants to rip us from the grasp of pride and release us into the freedom and peace of heart that a life set on him has in store. So how does God remove this grip of the serpent's bite? He allows our limitations to reveal the beauty of our poverty and need by teaching us lessons in virtue and humility.

But this is not done overnight. In fact, the *Catechism of the Catholic Church* tells us that "the education of the conscience is a lifelong task … [it] teaches virtue; it prevents or cures fear, selfishness and *pride*, resentment arising from guilt, and feelings of complacency, born of human weakness and faults. The education of the conscience *guarantees freedom and engenders peace of heart*" (CCC 1784, emphasis added). Perhaps it is time to let the Divine Teacher knock the forbidden apple out of our hands, clothe our consciences in humility, and rest our hearts in his freedom and peace.

> So how does God remove this grip of the serpent's bite? He allows our limitations to reveal the beauty of our poverty and need by teaching us lessons in virtue and humility.

So before we take a bite out of that rotten yet deceivingly tempting apple, maybe we should listen to a woman who faced her struggle with pride. A beautiful mother of seven, my lovely friend Emily Jaminet once found herself drowning in an exhausting and isolating sea of control. But then God stepped in. With a heart on fire for Christ's own Sacred Heart, Emily was rescued out of the lonesome boat of pride she once toiled in and was transformed and restored by the baptism of humility. It is my prayer that her reflective and tender words will unfix the apple from our gaze, help us drop the heavy oars of self-reliance, and rest in God's most perfect care.

Love Is Not Proud

EMILY JAMINET

Dear Younger Self,

As I pause for a minute and reflect on the last twenty-five years of marriage and seven beautiful children, I am in awe over the Lord's plan for your life. He has given you a "rich" life full of relationships, community, and experiences that have brought you a wealth of knowledge, love, and meaning. Be grateful, young one, for your vocation as wife and mother will lead you to the waters of both joy and suffering and draw you into the ocean of God's love. Motherhood offers you a road map to encounter the love of Christ through the humble road of service to God and others. The fruit of this journey is that your heart grows in its capacity to love and be loved as it is stretched, year in and year out.

But I need you to know something. There is so much that the Lord plans to teach you. It won't always be easy, and it certainly won't always be pretty. No, mama, it will be hard. But when the going gets tough, don't toss in the towel because you feel too weak, but rather turn to Christ for your strength. Sometimes, learning will be difficult, foreign, and even painful. Please don't slam the door of your heart to these difficult lessons. For when we stay engaged and willing, we grow and are strengthened.

You love, and oh, how you deeply love. You love hearing the little feet running through the house and, at times, even washing the muddy hands that have been playing outside in the sandbox and dirt. You love watching your children grow and try new things like sports and experiencing success. You love the man who not only shares their eyes and heart but accompanies the journey of parenting and life with you. You love this family you call your own, and with each new little member, it seems to grow like new branches on a tree.

This insidious thing called *pride* will place a murky veil over your love of Christ. It will prevent you from loving God and others.

But sweet girl, you also have a hidden and shrouded love. A love that you keep buried and tucked away from even your own eyes. A love that has resulted from the false belief that you are as good as you produce. It blurs your vision of truth as it has you laser-focused on your own achievements, your own esteem, your own way, your own glory. This concealed love is one of great danger and distraction. This insidious thing called *pride* will place a murky veil over your love of Christ. It will prevent you from loving God and others.

Pride brews in your heart, as you want to prove to yourself and the world that you can wife well, mother well, and "do it all" well. But just as pride was the sin that turned angels into devils, it can turn your selfless acts of love into self-serving transgressions. The Garden of Eden was the treasure we once had where the perfect exchange of love abounded. Yet, it is through the devil's planting of the seeds of pride that mankind ushered in "original sin" and experienced the great fall. Pride will similarly knock you off the firm ground of love if you let it.

So sweet one, it's time to begin the work in the garden of your own heart. It's time to gently begin plucking and weeding out this sin so that the disease of pride will not destroy the fruit of your labor, your marriage, and your motherhood. But the wound of pride does not stop there. It does more than injure the relationships of your vocation. It wounds your own heart and creates a distance from the most glorious heart of all—God's. Love, sweet one, is not prideful.

With your face held high in self-righteousness, pride prevents you from bowing your head to God and submitting to his will. So pay attention, dear one, and invite God into this garden you are blooming. Let him gently prune your overgrowth of pride so that you can remain a branch firmly abiding in him, the True Vine.

Your heart is so good and overflows with a desire to learn from Christ, to love like Christ. But did you know that, with all the lessons and witness of love that Jesus gave us while here on earth, he only explicitly said "learn from me" one time throughout Scripture? What did he want us to learn? In Matthew 11:29, Jesus tells us to learn from him "for I am gentle and lowly in heart." He could have said anything. He could have said *be generous, be patient, be honest*. But he didn't. Jesus was clear on what he wanted us to learn: to be gentle and humble. And lucky for you, sweet one, nothing will humble you quicker than the vocation of motherhood. It strips you of control, leaves you exposed to the messy, and reveals the bigness of your love and the littleness of your human frailty. As a wife and mother, you were crafted to be a life-bearer and life-giver. Yet, the poison of pride will only rot the fruit of your service, robbing you of living the beauty of your vocation. It will harden your heart and make you unresponsive to the true needs of those you love. Pride does not say sorry. But when you accept your poverty and need for God, humility will swiftly drop you to your knees in prayer and petition. And while you are down there, maybe look that little one in the eyes and ask for forgiveness.

Now, close your eyes and think of the beautiful painting that once hung in your grandparents' home and now rests on the walls of your parents' house. It is of a seaman in a boat making his way alone out to sea to a giant sailboat in the distance. This

man is working hard on a great adventure. He seems brave, competent, and heroic. For years, it will be easy to think that this is the ideal life: "me and my boat" or perhaps even "look at what I can do." You are tempted to think that this picture is the ideal way to move through life. You even secretly idolize this man for his strength and courage. But there is one important detail that you miss. He … is … all … alone; it is just him and his accomplishments. Pause, take a moment, and your exhausted eyes will see the risks of embracing this type of Rugged Individualism. This man, strong yet alone, needs help in this challenging task of rowing. He is only relying on himself. If he capsizes, who will save him? There is no one there to help guide him, steady the boat, or rescue him when the ocean's elements take him out of the security and safety that he once knew. When the raging storms come, which they will, there is no one to encourage him on his way or to take the lead when he is too weary to keep going. One unexpected and crushing wave will capsize his boat and swallow him up.

When I look at the little boat now, I wonder whether he may have rejected help to showcase his strength or to gain greater glory and praise. I like to ponder what could have been if he had made room for one more.

Oh, young one, I have a secret for you. There is no glory in rowing through life like the lone sailor. "I don't need anyone" and "I can do it by myself" do not make you heroic. No sweet one, they will only make you resentful, weary, and beaten down. Rowing alone in the boat of life demands focused attention on survival. And then, with your eyes down and hands anxiously grasping the oars, you will be robbed of seeing all the goodness and beauty that God has set out before you. Instead, learn to invest in your relationships and seek to discover and build an authentic community. Instead of rowing your boat alone, seek to steady your life by clinging to the large Mast in the center of the leading ship farther out. One of the bravest and strongest things you can do is to rest in humility and let yourself be loved and cared for by others. Reflect and see areas where you can build a greater community to support your mission to raise a large family.

*Oh, young one,
I have a secret for you.
There is no glory in rowing
through life like the lone sailor.*

I can see other areas in your life where this hidden pride rests deeply nestled in your heart. Your love for your children is so beautiful and so big. Yet your fear has left a foothold for pride to sneak its way into your motherhood. You frequently believe that your ways are the best ways. You often reject the loving advice of others about your children or family before you have even talked about it with your husband or prayed about it with God. You have rested on the idea that "Mother Knows Best" applies to all matters. You are slowly building a wall around your heart and home that is lonely and difficult to tear down.

I see you and know that you still carry sorrow in your heart from the years of embarrassment you endured when you struggled in school. It has locked up the gates of your heart. You rarely share your true needs and feelings. You have unknowingly imprisoned your freedom behind the walls of pride. You vow that you will no longer let others see your faults, your humanity, your poverty.

But I'm here to tell you that true freedom comes from revealing the fullness of your heart and receiving love in return. If this feels terrifying, begin with the most gentle lover of all, Christ himself. One day you will fall to your knees before the image of the Sacred Heart of Jesus and give the Lord "my marriage, my children, my life and my future." This small act will unlock the gates of your heart, and you will begin to let the Lord reveal the healing he has in store for you. He will slowly start to take down the walls of your heart, brick by brick. Jesus offers you his heart to burn off your sin with his perfect love. So sweet one, let him tear down those walls and let yourself be loved.

As you let God prune, tear down, and restore please remember one thing, Momma. You can't give what you don't have. You must live a healthy and happy life and pass on the fruit of your life. If you are not plugged into the love of God, you won't be able to be an instrument of passing that on to your children. Read in Scripture, "Love the Lord your God with all your heart, and with all your soul, and with all your mind, and with all your strength," and not forget to "love your neighbor as yourself" (Mark 12:30–31). Be able to have a heart like Christ's, meek and humble, and seek to have the Lord fill you up with his love so there is no room left to be prideful.

When you go to Mass, allow the Sacrament to refresh your soul no matter how hard parenting the children is. Don't carry the stress or burden of what others think of you and your family to impact your time at Mass. You will build a consistent and beautiful legacy by going to Mass year in and year out.

Lastly, recall that God has given you every day as a gift; remember that, so you don't waste the gift. Time is a blessing, especially time together with your family. Don't wish your life away! Yes, the seasons of life can be both joy-filled and difficult. You might be walking through a challenging time, so offer it to Jesus and grow nearer to him.

Make Christ's love the standard of your home, and ask him to remove the counterfeits of love, such as pride and stubbornness. That means your home needs to feel warm and a place where memories are made, work ethics reinforced, and tasks taught.

In Joshua, we read, "As for me and my house, we will serve the LORD" (Joshua 24:15). Make sure that your example is attractive to your husband and children, and when it isn't, seek more grace, ask for forgiveness and try again! Life is too short to be rowing our boat out at sea alone; instead, discover the true joy of the Gospel through loving and serving others.

All for Jesus,

YOUR FUTURE SELF

- PRAYER -

*Lord, I thank you for the fatherly pride
you have for the beauty and creation
of each and every soul.
Please help me to remember
and delight in my littleness.
Give me the docility to rest in knowing
that alone I am but a small grain of sand,
but that with you my soul
is fashioned to be as glorious
as the moon and stars and as big as the oceans.
When the temptation to prove
my worth blinds me from the beauty
and truth of my motherhood,
please remove my veil of pride
so that I can once again
see my children with
your loving eyes.*

Amen.

Love Honors Others

Woman's soul is ... fashioned to be a shelter in which other souls may unfold.

ST. TERESA BENEDICTA OF THE CROSS

The love of a mother is one of the most powerful forces known to mankind. We would slay the dragons, leap in front of the trains, and run into the burning buildings, or perhaps like Moses' mother, Jochebed, we may even lay our child in a papyrus basket among the reeds of a riverbank to protect him from harm. Like every protagonist in every fairytale ever written, our maternity blooms into a devotion to our beloveds of heroic proportion.

Even the seemingly minute and mundane become acts of motherly strength and fortitude. With every dish we wash, muddy shirt we clean, or sleepless night we endure, our maternal love makes way for the blood, sweat, and tears we willingly shed. Yet, when exhaustion, fear, and frustration take over, our words and actions frequently do not line up with the truth of our abounding maternal love. We grow impatient, lose our tempers, criticize, and unintentionally wound. We dishonor. How can this be? How can we be willing to fight to the ends of the earth for our children, yet crumble under the weight of a three-year-old temper tantrum?

To battle this disconnect, there are two questions that the Lord keeps placing within my heart and before my eyes time and time again. The first question is "Are you *for* them?", and I wholeheartedly answer "Yes!" But the deeper question that God asks is not only whether I am for them, but whether or not *they know it*. And it is with this that I pause. Do they?

We have been gifted with the honor of leading little hearts in love. Yet, many of us become consumed with the world's idea of success. Are they excelling in school, in their social settings, in their sport, in their club activities, and in their duties at home? We love them dearly and want them to succeed in life, and we surely don't want them to suffer! Yet, our children all too often suffer the greatest at the hands of one whose love has become wrapped up in fear and expectation—Momma.

Our children live in a world that is frequently against them. It won't fight for the good of their hearts, their identities, or their belovedness. Instead, it will feed them the lie that they are what they achieve; they must do more, be more, achieve more. Our maternal love must be willing to stand on the front lines of this battle, ready to combat the lies of the world with the shield and sword of God's truth.

And even when our hearts have been opened to the truth that our children are loved not for *what they do* but for *whose they are*, our words can still become darts that inflict pain and heartache. Even with a Christian worldview we can become overwhelmed and frustrated by our children's lack of virtue. Why aren't they selfless enough, obedient enough, honorable enough, gracious enough? So we critique, criticize, and unknowingly shame. This fractures their trust and deflates their confidence in their innate goodness. St. Paul so poignantly emphasizes the importance of honoring those we love with our words, "Let no evil talk come out of your mouths, but only such as is good for edifying, as fits the occasion, that it may impart grace to those that hear" (Ephesians 4:29). We must use the power of our words to affirm the truth in our children's hearts that we are and will always be in their corner.

One of the most fascinating roles found in the arena of sports is that of a boxer's cornerman. Much like a mother for a child, the cornerman plays a crucial yet often understated role. He does much more than provide physical support. During the fight, the cornerman must perceive the fighter's emotions and provide words of encouragement and advice that will best help the fighter remain motivated to stay in the game. Without the right cornerman, many boxers would be out of the game before the bell rings. So, too, we are called to be the all-important cornerman in the lives of our children.

St. John Paul II so beautifully emphasizes the beauty of this significant role we play in their lives. "Thank you, women who are mothers! You have sheltered human beings within yourselves in a unique experience of joy and travail. This experience makes you become God's own smile upon the newborn child, the one who guides your child's first steps, who helps it to grow, and who is the anchor as the child makes its way along the journey of life."[8]

I desire to be a reliable cornerman and anchor for the six little souls in my home, to receive their wounds, encourage their hearts, support their souls, and motivate them to fight the ultimate fight. But to be that place of honor for our children, we must remember the honor God bestowed upon our own hearts and souls.

> *My son, glorify yourself with humility,*
> *and ascribe to yourself honor according to your worth.*
> *Who will justify the man that sins against himself?*
> *And who will honor the man who dishonors his own life?*
> –Sirach 10:28–29

We are God's beloved. When we are clothed in the armor of this truth, we are better equipped to be a conduit of honor that unveils his love for our children. So how can we live out this monumental task of knowing our belovedness and in turn mothering with honor, dignity, and grace? My sweet friend Lisa Brenninkmeyer, mother of seven with an intense love for God and passion for his Living Word, tenderly speaks to the young-mom heart about honor and love. A convert to the Catholic Church, Lisa rests deeply on the truth of her belovedness and encourages each mother to combat the lies of the enemy and uphold the truth of her dignity. It is my prayer that her words will not only encourage a softening of our hearts and lips, but it will also help us to slay the dragons that are battling our own hearts. Then, perhaps one day, our children will bless us with their own words when they say, "She opens her mouth with wisdom, and the teaching of kindness is on her tongue" (Proverbs 31:26).

Love Honors Others

LISA BRENNINKMEYER

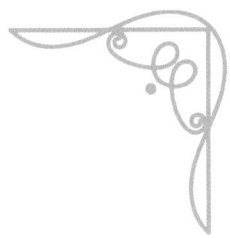

Hello, Love.

Can you put your list down for a moment, take a little break from the planning, and just sit with me? You don't have to check yourself in the mirror to see if you look OK, or move aside the clutter, or fluff the pillows on the couch. Just come as you are because it truly is good enough.

I'd love to talk with you right in the middle of the mess... not when you've made things as perfect as possible. You don't have to earn the right to take a little break. Don't clean things up for me; I know how hard it is to keep it all together.

I want you to know that I see you. I see all the effort you are making to bring your very best to the vocation of motherhood. It's what you've wanted to do with your life for as long as you can remember, and one baby has arrived after the other till your quiver got quite full. You got what you prayed for, and there is genuine gratitude spilling out of your heart. This is the career you have longed for, and you are doing all the reading, planning, organizing, and cleaning that could possibly be required. Four loads by four is the mantra for laundry. The goal for menu planning is to know what's for dinner by noon. You know not to expect what you don't inspect, so chore charts are being created and followed up on. These things do help it all go more smoothly. But are you inadvertently being lured onto a gerbil wheel of perfectionism? Are you afraid of what might happen if you try to get off? If you fail, does that make you a failure? Is your identity getting wrapped up in your performance?

I only ask because I notice that you look tired. And sometimes there's a little edge to your voice. You try to hide it well—that underlying frustration stemming from feeling *it is all up to you*. You know you need help, but even if you find the courage and humility to ask for it, you assume you'll just get another dose of high expectations from the people you love. But remember when your sensitive child looked up at your face and asked if you were OK? And you said that of course you were, but then he asked why your face looked like it was mad. They notice those little things. And they wonder if somehow it is their fault. This is the last thing you want any of them to feel.

I know this because I see the care you take with your words around them. Love doesn't dishonor others. Few things are as powerful in honoring or dishonoring as our tone and our words. Do they build up or tear down? Years ago, you read the verse, "Wisdom builds her house, but folly with her own hands tears it down" (Proverbs 14:1). You want to build a house where unconditional love flows through the rooms. The world is full of things that will tear your children and husband down, so you have done all you can to create an oasis at home where the verbal bruises are soothed, and the speaking of encouragement becomes a core memory. You know that one of the primary ways women tear down their own homes is through their bitter, harsh, complaining words. Children are like wet cement. Your words are imprinting on their brains in a way that will one day become their inner voice. Words matter. You know this.

> Children are like wet cement.
> Your words are imprinting on their brains in a way that will one day become their inner voice. Words matter.

But the load you carry feels heavy. The one who swept you off your feet, who wanted this big family as much as you did, who promised to make you happy for the rest of your life when you married him, he is often away from home.

Is resentment building in your heart? I think perhaps it is. Yes, he is providing for you all, but you feel he could be paying better attention to you. You aren't feeling happy, and didn't he promise to make sure that wouldn't be the case? If only he listened better. If only he didn't care so much about his job. If only he would just see that you need help and pitch in instead of waiting for you to fall apart. If only he could read your mind.

I know it is hard. This is a season of being pulled in so many directions, of exhaustion, of overwhelm. But can I gently ask you a few questions? Please don't hear judgment in my tone. I don't ask in that spirit. I'm coming alongside you to help draw you back to your deepest desire, which is to have a good, life-giving marriage. So I ask you, softly, how are your words about

him? If people formed their opinion of him based on the way you spoke about him to your girlfriends, what would they think of him? No one knows him better than you, after all. You are the guardian of your husband's reputation.

When he comes home, what does he see mirrored in your face? Joy, because he has walked through the door? Irritation, because he is late again? Indifference, because you've already been touched enough today? Do you know how much power your face holds over him? He wants to be who you want him to be. He is so afraid he isn't enough. Could it be that he is trying just as hard as you are? Might others' expectations feel as relentless to him as they do to you? Perhaps you both need somewhere to land softly and just *be*.

Even when you are weary, could you make the first move and let him land softly with you? Could you offer him the benefit of the doubt? To think the best of him instead of quickly attributing ill motive? To honor him with your love? Love doesn't dishonor others. To love is an action. It checks facial expressions. It pays attention to tone of voice. It moves across the room with a smile to give a hug and kiss even when it longs for solitude.

There will be days when you feel like you have given more than he has, and you might wonder why you should have to go the extra mile. Those are the times it's good to remember what you told your own daughter when she was struggling to do the right thing when those around her weren't particularly deserving of her kindness. Each morning, on the way to school, you encouraged her to live for an audience of One—to do the right thing, as if she were doing it for God himself—to remember that his approval was all that mattered. You wondered if she was really listening and doubted that she was. Her eyes were gazing out the window; her responses didn't make you feel like your words were very helpful. But you continued telling her about her worth, her identity, and the way that a daughter of the King should treat others.

You thought your heart would break the day of her birthday party. All your planning for a perfect celebration was undermined by a mean girl inviting everyone to come to a sleepover at her house after the party—everyone, that is, except your daughter. All the girls arrived with their pillows and sleeping bags and spoke of little else throughout the celebration. As you both drove home that afternoon, you asked her how she was feeling. How was her heart? Her response amazed you. She said, "I feel fine. I didn't do anything wrong at my party. God was happy with how I was treating

Treating others as if the Lord
was the One being served—as if he
was right there—because …
he actually is.

people. You told me to live for an audience of One. So I'm OK." Amazingly, she truly was. She had been listening. Your words were leaving a deep mark, a formative impression, even when it seemed like it was all going in one ear and out the other. Living for an audience of One. Treating others as if the Lord was the One being served—as if he was right there—because ... he actually is.

So should all the resentment and hurt just get stuffed down? Is the only way through to ignore feelings, to plaster on a facial expression that doesn't reflect the state of the heart, to speak positively and never let on that you are dying inside? Oh no. That is not the way forward. I know you have tried this. And on some level, it does seem to work. It works as far as outward appearances go. But on the heart level? That is another matter.

Love doesn't dishonor others. Do you know who else that applies to? You. If you are supposed to love your neighbor as yourself (see Mark. 12:31), then loving yourself must matter. A couple of things need to be held in balance. They may seem mutually exclusive, but I encourage you to hold all these things in tension. So you might consider practicing both/and thinking with thoughts like these: "I am BOTH devoted to my children AND I save time and energy each day for my spouse." "I am BOTH committed to my family AND I schedule time for solitude so I can pray." "I am determined to BOTH be available to my loved ones AND I prioritize spending time with life-giving girlfriends." The needs of your children matter, and your love must honor them. The needs of your husband matter, and your love must honor him. And your needs matter, so effort needs to be made to honor yourself. You are God's beloved daughter. You are not a workhorse. He cares deeply about how your heart is doing. He sees your needs and does not want them to be ignored.

By this, I don't mean he wants you to become obsessed with self-love and self-care. It's not so much about getting a massage, having a bubble bath, or always saying no if something feels inconvenient. It's a matter of paying attention to what is going on in your mind and heart and being honest about it. It's paying attention to your body—to the times when your shoulders are tight, your stomach is upset, your head is aching. It's taking the time to ask yourself what you are feeling, and reminding yourself that feelings aren't right or wrong, they just are. It's paying attention to negative self-talk in your head and replacing those thoughts with life-giving, honoring truths. When you pay attention to those things inside you, you can make loving decisions about how to meet the needs you truly have and how to provide for the things others need from you.

If you will commit to the practice each day, journaling can really be a game-changer for you. It will give you a chance to do the work of comparing what is in your head with what God says is true. The starting point is to get all the garbage out on the paper. No editing. No worrying that someone is going to read it. Just let it all pour out.

Once you're done, you can take a step back and think about your thoughts. Ask God to help you identify any lie-based thinking. Are any of these lies woven through your thoughts?

I'm all alone.
I am stuck.
I am defined by my failures.
God doesn't care.
It's all up to me.

Or are you overgeneralizing—applying one experience and generalizing it to all experiences? Are you catastrophizing? Are you blaming? Can you find the word "should" in your writing—evidence that you feel you must do something because it meets someone's expectations of you?

As you work through this process of "thinking about what you think about," it's important to invite God into the experience. That's what turns journaling time into prayer instead of self-analysis. You can ask God to shed light on what is going on inside of you. You can ask him, "Is what I am thinking about myself or my circumstances consistent with *your* perspective, Lord? Is it consistent with what I have learned from Scripture, or does it contradict it?" Take a few moments to sit in silence, asking him to shed light on your concerns. Jot down any insights.

Sometimes you will find that this is all you need to bring your heart back into alignment. But other times you will discover that for your heart to be honored, things need to change. You will have to grow in your ability to speak "the truth in love" (Ephesians 4:15). Love doesn't dishonor others. It communicates respectfully and charitably, but also honestly. This is not easy. It takes a tremendous amount of courage. But the alternative is stuffing emotions, which leads to bitterness and resentment. No matter how much you might try to hide this behind a façade of good performance and perfect homemaking, those things will leak out. Always, without fail. Honor yourself, honor your marriage, honor your vocation as a mother by being willing to forgo harmony temporarily in order to work toward solutions that are best for everyone. Be brave and truthful. Fight for your heart. Remember that artificial harmony isn't real. It's worth it to go through a short period of conflict to get to the root of the matter. Don't wait twenty years to do this. Time will be lost.

Your heart is beautiful and has a tremendous capacity to give. Fill it with what is supernatural, and what you share will be transforming in its power.

Joy will be forfeited. Press into this honest communication and your heart will be better for it. I promise. And you won't be the only one to benefit—this will be modeled for your children for their future relationships and create a more peace-filled home during their childhoods.

Your heart is beautiful and has a tremendous capacity to give. Fill it with what is supernatural, and what you share will be transforming in its power. Jesus said, "Out of the abundance of the heart his mouth speaks" (Luke 6:45). Go to the source of divine love and ask God to fill your heart with all that it needs, and not stop pouring in until it overflows. Let that overflow be what you give your family. It'll be more potent than your human love. Your words will become infused with encouragement that delivers comfort, truth that bestows dignity, and love that honors those dearest to you.

With Love,
YOUR FUTURE SELF

– PRAYER –

*My sweet Jesus, thank you
for speaking blessings over me.
In a world that frequently hurts, shames,
rejects, and criticizes, I have found refuge
in your loving embrace.
Please give me the strength to be soft,
the courage to surrender, and the endurance
to pursue all that is good, especially in my motherhood.
Please rid my mouth of the words that will hurt,
and take from my heart the thoughts
that will breed anger and resentment.
Instead, I pray that my words, my voice,
and my heart will be a source of life
for the little loves in my home.
For "pleasant words are like a honeycomb,
sweetness to the soul and health to the body"
(Proverbs 16:24).*

Amen.

Love Does Not Insist on Its Own Way

> Jesus deigned to show me the road that leads to this divine furnace, and this road is the surrender of the little child who sleeps without fear in its father's arms. "Whoever is a little one, let him come to me."
>
> ST. THÉRÈSE OF LISIEUX

Mothers everywhere have a deep, albeit sometimes hidden, desire to mother well, regardless of whether or not we rise to the challenge. Motherhood came earlier than expected for some, later than planned for others, and without enough guidance and support for most. Many women all over the world have been tempted to wave their white flags and retreat from pursuing the ideals of love in motherhood.

But then many have not retreated.

Many have accepted the invitation to create a home full of love, beauty, and goodness. Resolved to love their children well, many women have chased after a holy and wholesome motherhood with every ounce of their being. We want to do it right. I want to do it right.

But below the surface of this selfless pursuit of good is a sentiment that often takes over the wheel of my motherhood journey and redirects me off the path of love—a powerful four-letter word—FEAR. The fear of failure may be the greatest concern buried deep in a mother's heart. We don't want to mess up. I don't want to mess up. So fear comes along and swallows us alive. And anyone who has ever sat in the belly of the whale of fear knows that all too often our method of escaping this

desperate and dark place is *control*. We will dig ourselves out, we will fight the giant fish, we will fix it all, and we will do it *our* way. When the fear of failure begins to swallow and suffocate us, we do what we think we must—we try longer, try smarter, try harder. Try, try, try!

"*This* is how they should be fed, socialized, educated, and catechized. This is what is best for them!" But often God steps in and calls us in a new direction. He may ask us to stop planning every part of the journey or may even invite us down an entirely new road. But tired and afraid, we seek our plans, our way, and puffed up with control, we run away from all that God has in store.

Similarly, exhausted and fearful, Jonah fled from God and his sovereign plans. Seeking himself and his ways did nothing but bring the raging seas upon Jonah and his shipmates. And it is in seeking our own ways that we, too, bring the turbulent storms onto the shipmates of our own lives—our children. The very ones we are afraid of hurting become the ones stuck in the sinking boat with us.

When we realize the destruction that has sometimes ensued, we may be tempted to throw ourselves overboard, just as Jonah did. But sweet momma, before you do that, let's take a lesson from Jonah, who quite literally sat in the stenchy belly of a whale. He released the grip of control, lifted his fears to the Divine Captain, and surrendered everything ...

> *"The waters closed in over me,*
> *the deep was round about me;*
> *weeds were wrapped about my head*
> *at the roots of the mountains.*
> *I went down to the land*
> *whose bars closed upon me for ever;*
> *yet you brought up my life from the Pit,*
> *O Lord my God.*
> *When my soul fainted within me,*
> *I remembered the Lord;*
> *and my prayer came to you ..."*
> *And the Lord spoke to the fish,*
> *and it vomited out Jonah upon the dry land.*
> –Jonah 2:5–7, 10

This is where the beauty of a poor and surrendered heart lies. We see in Jonah that rather than hiding, trying, and drowning in our plans, real freedom comes from remembering, praying, and being rescued by *his*.

But how can we, like Jonah, relinquish control and let the docility of his perfect love take the wheel? It begins by first recognizing how we subtly seek ourselves rather than the ways of the One who never stops seeking us. This is a lesson that my dear friend Elizabeth Foss, with a heart after Christ's, slowly learned through her patient pursuit of love. With a desire to remake the story that her own childhood once told the world, this homeschooling momma of eight ferociously pursued the good, beautiful, and true, both in her home and outside. But underneath this drive to do better was an incredible fear of failure. The worry that she wasn't enough for the story that God wanted to write with her life left heavy chains upon her shoulders. Yet, after many years, tears, and hours on her knees, God slowly transformed her heart and helped her release the grip that fear and control once had on her.

Through her tender words, Elizabeth gently scoops up the heart of her young and weary self, the heart of many of us, and tenderly asks her to let go of this drive to *do* well and instead *be* well resting in his most perfect care. So it is my prayer that the next time you are overshadowed by worry and control, Elizabeth's words will help you breathe, surrender, and remember *him*. And maybe, like Jonah, you lift your eyes and heart to the heavens, ask God to spit you out of the giant abyss of fear, and remember, "Many are the plans in the mind of a man, but it is the purpose of the Lord that will be established" (Proverbs 19:21).

Love Does Not Insist on Its Own Way

ELIZABETH FOSS

Hey, Sweet Girl!

You've got your hands full, don't you? It's going to be ok. Let's talk.

You are so far beyond tired; you're wiped out, burned out, tapped out, and certainly touched out. You spend your days serving your people—this little band of boys and girls who are everything you ever wanted. But there are so many of them and not nearly enough of you. Before these children arrived, you dedicated yourself to learning everything you could about children—about educating them, parenting them, and counseling them. You even have an oversized degree from a fancy school to prove how well-prepared you were for this grand adventure. And it wasn't all academic. No, you've read deeply about the treasure of the Church. You think you have a full understanding of the Theology of the Body and sacred openness to life. You've spent hours and hours on your knees begging for the chance to create a beautiful family together with God. When you welcomed these wee ones into your life, you did it with every intent to lay down your life for them.

And now, you are overwhelmed. You don't want to admit it because you still believe with all your heart that children are always and only a blessing. So, you think that the problem must be that you are inadequate. You have such a vision for abundant life—a loving marriage, good and holy children, and a beautiful, welcoming home—but somehow, you just can't make it come to be. Everywhere you look, you see evidence of your imperfections. You believe that God has called you to an abundant life in him, and you believe that it is what he wants for you (see John 10:10). But life doesn't feel joyfully abundant at all. It feels broken and disjointed, and since God is God, you figure the problem lies with you. You must be doing it wrong.

You feel torn. You're giving full time and attention to your children, trying mightily to make solid, loving attachments with them, to steward the individual gifts of each of them, to love them deeply and well. And you're doing your very best, under your own strength, to make your home a soft place to land. You're mindful of finances. You think you're drawing upon every last bit of creativity you have with an eye toward beauty and comfort. You've read all the home management books. And we both know you've created more chore charts than the major airlines have created flight plans. Children: check. Home: check. Neither situation is up to your ideals, but you keep climbing Sisyphus' mountain, relentless in your pursuit of perfection.

And then there is your husband.

Co-creator of this bountiful brood. He's working so hard, trying so hard, building a career while building a family. You have perfunctory conversations about carpools and soccer coaches and picking up dog food on the way home. You can't remember the last time you set aside a chunk of time to just laugh together. He's your best friend, your strongest support, your most ardent ally, your tender comfort—and you miss him terribly.

You feel like you're failing everything. Despite your best efforts, nothing is measuring up to your ideal. You want to be an excellent

wife. You want to be the very best mother your kids could hope to have. You want to be a proficient and thoughtful homemaker. You want to be dependable and shine in your apostolates outside your home. And—despite all your encouragement as a champion for mothers who choose to forego outside employment in favor of staying home with kids—you also really want to be good at your job.

I whisper to you, dear sweet girl who tries so hard: *stop self-seeking.*

You want. You want. You want. You want. You want.

Don't you see? You are insisting on your own way. You are on a quest for what you want. And it's so sneaky, so very tricky. The enemy has twisted up your good and holy calling and distorted it so that you can't quite hear God's voice over the interior clamor of perfectionism, leading you just ever so slightly away from the path God wants to walk with you.

You think that you are being anything but insisting on your own way. In reality, you are most definitely questing after your own desires, your own idyllic vision. And therein lies your utter exhaustion.

I whisper to you, dear sweet girl who tries so hard: *stop self-seeking.*

And you are indignant.

I hear you protesting. *Oh! But I don't insist on my own way! I am wholly oriented toward the needs of my children. I am fully focused on forming beautiful souls for Christ. I have completely abandoned my own wants and needs. I'm all in for them. I'm laying down my life for my family! What more could anyone possibly want from me?*

And I smile at you tenderly.

Laying down your life for your family doesn't mean killing yourself. It doesn't mean beating yourself into oblivion and stumbling through every day, exhausted and burned out. You, my friend, are pursuing a false martyrdom of your own making.

Looking for inspiration, you are tempted by the little squares. You scroll through the beautiful pictures. You read captions full of holy inspiration. For a few moments, you feel a rush of hope, a hit of encouragement. And then it happens. Shame. An overwhelming feeling of inadequacy washes over you. Taken together, you see evidence in the little squares that it is possible to create excellence in all parameters of life. *They do.*

But not you. You fall short. At night, in the dark, before you fall asleep, you joke with your husband that when you die, your headstone will read, "She tried." But hot, quiet tears run down your face and onto your pillow. It's no laughing matter.

I cup your face in my hands, brushing away your tears with my thumbs.

Our good, good Father wants you to offer your life to him. He wants you to stop trying so hard and start trusting. Yielding. Surrendering. He wants you to stop white-knuckling your way through your days and instead unclench your fists and open your hands to his grace and his mercy.

Sweet girl, you have been insistent on your own way. You've read the books, listened to the talks, and followed the holy influencers. And you think you have this whole thing figured out. So, you insist on this way, even though this way is leaving you irritable and resentful all the time, whether you acknowledge it or not. While we're here in this pain point, let me whisper something from the future for you: all the irritation and resentment that you won't voice and won't even admit to yourself is a very fine fertilizer for bitterness when these children are grown and gone. Now is the time to learn to really love the way God intends you to love.

God calls you to love your husband and your children as you love yourself. Tell me, sweet girl, do you love yourself? Do you truly believe that you are, indeed, enough? Enough for your husband, to fill his cup with all the good things that only you can offer? Enough for your children, to guide and teach and heal and nurture? Enough for your friends and your community to not only create a place of welcome but to actually be a person of genuine life-giving hospitality?

Or do you think that you have to be perfect to be loved?

You believe you are carrying the cross the Lord chose especially for you, but I am reminding you that he said that his yoke is easy and his burden is light (see Matthew 11:28–30). This load you carry all day, and even at night, it's neither easy nor light. It's cumbersome and burdensome and you feel very alone under the suffocating weight of it. That promise of a yoke that suits you and you alone? It's not just for other people. That promise is for you, too. You don't have to stagger under the weight of trying to be perfect anymore.

You are insisting on bringing your idyllic vision to life under your own power. You are self-seeking. And here is how you know that for sure: The thoughts you are thinking—your daily dialogue with yourself—fuels impatience and resentment. You are well on your way to reaping a life of bitterness instead of blessing.

True love doesn't have to be perfect; it just has to be true.

You don't have to be perfect; you just have to be true. Be true to who God created you to be. Get to know yourself. Don't be afraid of your weaknesses. They don't mean that you are broken.

**You don't have to be perfect;
you just have to be true.
Be true to who God created you to be.**

The weak places, the cracks in your shiny veneer? Those are the places God fills with himself, crafting you into a vessel of love more beautiful than the most exquisite Japanese kintsugi pottery; it's the gold-filled cracks that make it beautiful. God himself can be the gold in your broken places.

And childhood doesn't have to be perfect. You ran so hard and so fast from the unhappy, unhealthy home of your own growing up that you think you have to create the perfect life for your children. You don't. Healthy homes are homes where mistakes can be made and children learn that they are loved even when they mess up. You do that for them; now do it for yourself. It's OK when you hit a bump or you stumble or you fall flat on your face. You are still loved. Know that you are loved. Behave as if you are loved. Relax into that love and then let it grow inside of you.

To truly educate your children well in the school of love, stop trying to be all the things to all the people. Instead, admit your shortcomings. Tell them you don't have all the answers. Be fully awake to see where God shows up in your doubts and your weaknesses. Look for all the ways God pours himself into the gaps (often using other people to cooperate and collaborate with us) and be astounded by graciousness. He is sufficient.

Finally, sweet girl, fix your eyes on God. Stop striving and perfecting and performing for other people. You are serving because you are seeking approval and affection; stop making that your motivation, because that, my love, is the hidden self-serving. Engrave magnanimity upon your heart. (Or wear it on your wrist: put it where you are always, always reminded.) To be magnanimous is to truly grow in honest love in such a way that you possess genuine greatness of soul. No longer serving because you are seeking something for yourself, you will behave with nobility because your actions come from a deep well of God's own love. You know it. It animates you. That love is who you are, and it is whose you are. You rest in it. And you fully awake and fully alive is the abundant life he richly bestows on you.

With much tender love,

A GRAYER, SOFTER, WISER YOU

- PRAYER -

*Lord, thank you for the incredible gift of YOU
and your most perfect care.
Please help me to remember that you,
the King of Heaven and Earth, who has offered yourself fully,
even to the point of death—death on the Cross,
are the sovereign king of both my heart and home.
My Jesus, please give me the docility to release
the grasp of control and self-seeking.
Help me to entrust my children to your divine care
so that I may experience the peace of fully believing
and trusting the truth of your words.
"For my thoughts are not your thoughts,
neither are your ways my ways
... For as the heavens are higher than the earth,
so are my ways higher than your ways
and my thoughts than your thoughts"
(Isaiah 55: 8-9).*

Amen.

Love Does Not Become Angry Easily

Contemplation is nothing else but a secret, peaceful, and loving infusion of God, which, if admitted, will set the soul on fire with the Spirit of love.

ST. JOHN OF THE CROSS

Ohhh, *Anger*. This five-letter word often trips up the best-intentioned mommas. With gritty teeth and red-hot faces, we frequently find ourselves mumbling, grumbling, groaning, or yelling out against the believed injustices we've experienced at the hands of tots through teens. Then, when the water of our soul stops boiling, we shrink back in regret and heartache. "Why did I have to yell again?", "Why did those words come out of my mouth?" This shame is the precise place in which the enemy can grip his claws into the fleshy heart of a mother.

The *Catechism of the Catholic Church* explains that anger, which is "a desire for revenge," is clearly prohibited when it is motivated by a vengeant desire "to do evil to someone who should be punished." However, it goes on to explain that righteous anger is, in fact, praiseworthy, for it imposes "restitution to correct vices and maintain justice" (CCC 2302). Many times throughout Scripture, the King of the World, our good and perfect Father, expressed anger—that is, his righteous anger. Jesus himself threw over tables and scolded those who robbed the sacred Temple of its honor and reverence. But, sweet mommas, how different our anger often is. We desire so deeply to love well, yet in the chaos of life, we frequently become angry quickly, easily, and unrighteously. And Scripture warns us of this, "Let every man be quick to hear, slow to speak, slow to anger" (James 1:19).

Perhaps one of the reasons we are so quick to be short-tempered, disgruntled, or angry is that we forget that God is Lord of our lives. We frequently see interruptions, while God sees invitations. We feel exhaustion, while God sees stretching and strengthening. We perceive disobedience and meltdowns, while God sees the building of patience and security. Perhaps we plan the right way, while God sees the *best* way, *his* way.

God desires to take us on a path that
leads to the greatest and most
divine joy, that of communion with him.

Though it may not always be pretty, easy, or seemingly uninterrupted, God desires to take us on a path that leads to the greatest and most divine joy, that of communion with him. Yet, unbeknownst to ourselves we frequently fight with everything we have against the plans of the Lord. God wants us to know that he is in our midst, and perhaps, a Bible story about a prophet and his talking donkey may just be what we need to remember that God is present and active in our lives.

Balaam, a prophet from Moab, was esteemed for being a soothsayer who could bless or curse with his words. Despite living amongst idolaters, Balaam professed his knowledge of the one true God. Yet still, with a self-seeking heart, he decided to obey the Moabite King's request that he curse the Israelites. As Balaam rode toward the Israelites, his donkey suddenly swerved off route. What the donkey could see, while the hardened heart of Balaam could not, was that an angel of the Lord was blocking their path. Balaam, determined to complete his assignment, was blind to the angel's presence. So he beat his donkey, commanding that he stay on route. But once again the donkey swerved off their path, and Balaam once again beat him. Then, when the angel moved in a narrow place leaving no room to swerve left

or right, the donkey simply stopped and lay down under Balaam himself. This enraged the prophet:

> Balaam's anger was kindled, and he struck the donkey with his staff. Then the Lord opened the mouth of the donkey, and she said to Balaam, "What have I done to you, that you have struck me these three times?" … Then the Lord opened the eyes of Balaam, and he saw the angel of the Lord standing in the way, with his drawn sword in his hand; and he bowed his head, and fell on his face. And the angel of the Lord said to him, "Why have you struck your donkey these three times? Behold, I have come forth to withstand you, because your way is perverse before me." (Numbers 22:27–28, 31–32, emphasis added)

God was leading him off a path of destruction, but all that Balaam could see was a disobedient donkey, an interrupted journey, and an inconvenience to *his* plans. How often are we just like Balaam, with our eyes so focused on behavior, disrupted plans, or messy homes, that we forget that the King of the World's work is at hand? He is at work in the nursery, at the kitchen sink, throughout the hustle and bustle of the day, and in the little ones who both spill the milk and snuggle up in our laps as the day nears an end. He is even at work within the heart of a mother who abounds and is stretched by love, who whispers affirmations and yells with regret. He delights in her goodwill to love tenderly and envelops her with mercy when she doesn't.

The days are long, and the years are hard, magnificently beautiful, but hard. Anger will come, and the tears will flow. So how can we mothers learn to slow down enough to recognize our Lord alive in our midst? How can we turn that anger into a time of reflection, contemplation, and intimacy with him? How can we invite Jesus in to help us explore the deeper source of our anger? And how can we know the mercies of God when,

He is even at work within the heart of a mother who abounds and is stretched by love, who whispers affirmations and yells with regret. He delights in her goodwill to love tenderly and envelops her with mercy when she doesn't.

like Balaam, we fall on our faces in regret and sorrow? Perhaps Christine Dudley, a beautiful mother of seven, can show us what it means to grow and stretch in maternal love. As a mother who has journeyed through the unthinkable heartache of losing her young child, Christine tenderly reminds us that this job of mothering is both hard and beautiful. It is my prayer that her words will breathe life into the heart of any mother who believes the lie that she is the *only one* who has let her anger spill into her home. I hope you will experience the solidarity she elicits as well as the encouragement her words provide as we learn to breathe throughout our maternity. For God tells us, "He who is slow to anger is better than the mighty, and he who rules his spirit than he who takes a city" (Proverbs 16:32).

Love Does Not Become Angry Easily

CHRISTINE DUDLEY

Dear Younger Self,

"Mama, you aren't a friend of Jesus because you yell too much." I see you taking in this statement from your guileless six-year-old son already with one foot in heaven. Like a swift kick to the gut, the words take your breath away. I see your mind racing, "Wait! I am a friend of Jesus! He is my strength and my hope. He is my all! And, dear, sweet, child of mine who I love so much, your impression of me is that I yell too much?" Flooding your mind, the events of the last few years topple over each other looking for footing. There they are…moving an hour away from parish, friends, and family, birthing seven children in 15 years, and caring for a child in the process of dying from brain cancer. Yes, you at your best and also at your worst.

Dearest, in an effort to understand, I see you scanning all the way back to the beginning. Your beginning and your beginning as a mother. You never wanted to have anger in your house. Remembering the seemingly constant bickering haunts your experience of family like ghosts floating into and out of your daily experience. Sitting on your front stoop leaning your head against the brick wall while your three littlest ride circles in the driveway, I see you despair that you used yelling as a tool. This is not who you want to be … "Why? Why am I that way?" you ask. Encouraging cooperation through collaborative problem solving, natural consequence instead of punishment, affirmation of feelings…the summarized titles of well-worn chapters in books crowd your mind. It works. The techniques work…and they don't. I see how much you do not want to be this way.

The truth is, Dear One, the job is hard. If anger is a clue to what is going on inside there are so many reasons. Conversations with mothers wiser than you, masters of generating intrinsic motivation, reveal their own struggles and creative efforts to plant seeds of being considerate of others, jars to fill, charts to check, and new systems to try. Over and over the pace races until there is a collapse of mother in mind and spirit. A line is crossed. The fourteenth time in an hour a line is crossed. There is no more room to absorb more. The limit is reached…and something comes from your mouth that you would never think possible. Shame, criticism, blame, an outpouring of emotion using your position of power to intimidate and crush their unruly spirit.

But…no one cries at your angry outburst. They do the thing. The anger is effective. It works. They move. In that moment, the intractable problem is solved. Then you say another horrible thing. You ask them why they make you yell. Why are they making you behave this way by not doing the thing until you yell? Oh, Dearest…what have you become? Not the mother you wanted to be. Not the image of God you want to be in their lives. It is hard. The best of parenting would be to not yell. Think ahead of what they are going to do…they always do the same things, so think about possible consequences, define the problem with them, brainstorm potential solutions, and create and sign contracts. The messy truth is, Dear One, you do all these things. You do the best of parenting and the worst. Both things are true. It is a hard job. Courageously resisting the temptation to rule with power and teaching them to do the same is the challenge.

> You do the best of parenting and the worst. Both things are true. It is a hard job.

What is left, Dear One? You had a dream of being the perfect parent. A narrative that said, "If I just did things right, had the right systems, held God in my heart in the right way, knew my own strengths and weaknesses, developed best practices, and followed them, there would always be harmony. No angry outbursts would emerge because we would be validating feelings, learning from each other, disagreeing to build relationship." Dear One, what your little ones, middle ones, and old ones need is the gift of apology.

You are not perfect. You will not ever be perfect. They won't ever be perfect either. When you cannot teach them to regulate their anger by your example, teach them how to accept responsibility. Teach them to say, "I am sorry. It's not your fault. I am working on not saying mean things. Know that I love you." At this moment, what is left is rebuilding the trust. A humble acknowledgment that you are as much a work in progress as anyone. It is not their fault. Your anger is not their fault. Never their fault.

The beautiful thing about having so many children over such a long period of time, Dear One, is your ability to keep practicing! To keep learning. You still have a child who tries you. Pushes you. Argues about doing her work. Does not do what she says she will. Naturally, she cannot do these things yet. Hauntingly one more time it is your job to make her feel the consequences of her choices while there is still time. This is holy work. And you will fail. There is disharmony. You argue when you shouldn't. Shame when you shouldn't. Blame when you shouldn't. You are better and you are still growing. The temptation to get big when she disagrees is as real as when the oldest disagreed. This time, Dear One, breathe in, breathe out. Love the little one inside of you who feels scared and threatened because disagreement might mean something horrible. This is a new moment. Teach this child of yours something new. Teach her to pause. To breathe

in. Breathe out. In this new moment, you become something new too. Raising these children is as much or even more about you growing up as it is about them.

Dear One, as I watch you, there is more to your anger than overwhelm in the moment. There is unavoidable burden buried and borne without respite. Moments and seasons where four cereal bowls hit the floor morning after morning. Months where the crying would not stop and naps would not be taken. No malice, no intent to disobey or procrastinate. Simple need manifested in the natural way and you, Dear One, with your mother's heart, met the need even if you were tired, at your limit, and confused about why it was hard. You did these things almost always with another new life growing within you or holding, soothing, and feeding the new life that recently arrived. It was hard. Something died within you. Numbing yourself to the overwhelm, you absorbed so much loss. It was both too

Raising these children
is as much or even more about you
growing up as it is about them.

much and it was the only way. Fear of conflict and failure led to your silent suffering, which led to bitterness. Budding confusion and frustration over why it had to be so hard. Why was such a subjectively and objectively good thing so hard? Was there a way to do this thing without becoming a shell of myself? Dear One, I am here ... I am holding you. This latent disappointment and anger are your pain. Absorbed in the moment, buried in your heart, waiting to emerge unexpectedly, desperately needing healing. Feel my love for you. You did so well! You did so much! You have a beautiful family. It was hard and it was good.

Being a mother of many is like a snake swallowing a meal. It is so much, done so intensely. And then it is over. What remains are the rents in your heart where you had to put others first beyond your capacity. Within you is a part who bore the burden and needs to cry about how hard it was. Many things are true, Dear One. You did your job. You did it well. It did hurt you to do it.

Dear One, the most important thing I want you to know is you are already an amazing mother. For all the times you see yourself losing your temper, I see a dozen where you watch with wonder and joy. From the toddler who crawls on the counter to eat the stick of butter and you telling yourself they must need more fat in their diet to the creative expression on the walls made with markers, crayons, and Vaseline. From the uncanny ability of your brood of little ones to break almost everything to the apparent inability to stop stuffing socks and really all clothing into the cushions of the furniture. All this you watched with curiosity.

The time is coming, Dear One, though you cannot see it yet, when you will wonder if you have wasted your life raising these children. The idea will burst into your psyche when a daughter tells you she wants to be a mother. Horrified she would limit her life and impact in the world in this way, you wonder, "What have I done? Have I just spent my life making more mothers?!? I thought I was sacrificing my life for lives that were going to do something amazing ... bigger than me. And now they will be small like me. What have I done?" I know in this moment you question your sacrifice and wonder if your decision was wise.

Mothering is an exercise in planned obsolescence. If you do your job effectively, you will no longer be needed. If you do your job, they will feel comfortable being honest about the pain you caused them through your own immaturity. As painful as it is to invest in a vocation that ends in being critiqued and unneeded, Dear One, I can confidently confess raising your children is the greatest adventure of your lifetime. There is nothing that preceded it or follows that will compare. Yes, Dear One, you will have meaningful work when they are gone and realize with growing confidence all the skills you honed running a small logistics company that is a family. And, still, nothing will compare with the priceless joy of watching a smile break across a face or the innocent abandonment of someone climbing higher than they have before. Nothing compares with the awe of witnessing a child comfort a companion, frost a cake, fix their car, or snake out their sink drain. Drink in your beautiful people with their strengths and challenges. When you feel your anger rise, breathe in. Breathe out. Remember, God loves you. The child who courageously said you were not a friend of Jesus is smiling and loving you, too.

Holding you in the light now and always,
YOUR OLDER SELF

- PRAYER -

*My loving Father, thank you for showering me
with an unending kind of love.
When I find myself swallowed up
by the shame of my mistakes,
lost temper, angry voice,
or irritated tone, please help me
remember your endless mercy.
Please give me the grace to
look the little people in the eyes,
ask for forgiveness, and rest in
your compassionate embrace.
Help me to recall the impact of my anger.
A harsh word stirs up anger, but a
gentle answer turns away wrath (see Proverbs 15:1).
I pray that with your help, I can learn to soften my face,
quiet my voice, and become an
embodiment of your gentle love.*

Amen.

Love Does Not Keep a Record of Wrongs

And when night comes, and you look back over the day and see how fragmentary everything has been, and how much you planned that has gone undone, and all the reasons you have to be embarrassed and ashamed: just take everything exactly as it is, put it in God's hands and leave it with Him. Then you will be able to rest in Him—really rest—and start the next day as a new life.

ST. TERESA BENEDICTA OF THE CROSS

Memories are a funny thing. Taking shape as our brains' neurons go about their activity, memories play a major role in how we perceive the world.[9] As we repeat a behavior, connections are reinforced in the brain and memories become stronger. These stronger memories are the ones we are more easily able to recall, impacting the movements of not only our hands and feet but frequently our hearts. But it isn't only the most repeated experiences that make solid homes in the mansion of our minds. Rather, as part of a protective survival tactic, our brains

will retain emotionally intense and painful memories longer than others. Our wounded hearts quite literally make it harder for our impressionable brains to forget the heartaches we both receive and impose.[10]

Yet, we so desperately try to muscle the will to overlook and forget offenses. We try to overlook the slammed door, the teenage eye roll, or even that child who threw their peanut butter and jelly sandwich on the floor because it wasn't cut to the high-maintenance specifications of this two-year-old.
But we mommas often find it much harder to overlook our own

errors. Our perfection-seeking hearts begin to tally up how we don't measure up, secretly keeping score of all that we have failed to accomplish or complete. We frequently become so consumed with all that our perfectly crafted checklist requires of us that our idolization of making things look just *right* turns our hearts oh so *wrong*. Our souls are left exposed and vulnerable to the hidden shame and self-condemnation that comes from focusing on our imperfections, and all too often this shame bubbles up and over onto those around us.

Martha, like many of us, was "anxious and troubled about many things" (Luke 10:41). Opening her home to the King of the World, her frustration at the less-than-perfect not only yielded anxiety over her inadequacies but also an outspoken condemnation for her sister who failed to meet *her* high standard of entertaining, a standard Jesus never set. Jesus reminds her, "One thing is needful. Mary has chosen the good portion" (Luke 10:42). But, sweet mommas, we must be clear here. It was NOT her serving that was the problem. No, that was a beautiful outpouring of self. Instead, it was making an idol of her perfect performance that robbed her from loving and receiving the love poured out by Perfection himself.

Perhaps, like Peter, it isn't just our less-than-perfect service that has us weeping bitterly. Maybe it's intense remorse and shameful regret for how we have hurt ourselves or our children. But Jesus came to unlock us from the grip of shame and self-condemnation and restore us to freedom in him. "There is therefore now no condemnation for those who are in Christ Jesus" (Romans 8:1).

Condemnation for ourselves or others has the power to destroy—destroy confidence, destroy love of self, destroy relationships, and even destroy life itself. Judas, consumed with shame, self-hatred, and self-condemnation, hung himself. Peter, full of sorrow, fished. And when the disciple John, recognizing the risen Jesus approaching the boat, screamed, "It is the Lord!"—Peter, fully clothed, "sprang into the sea" (John 21:7). In his childlike way, with repentance and sorrow, Peter ran to Jesus. And it was through Jesus' question, "Do you love me?" and Peter's resounding answer "Yes, Lord; you know that I love you," that his heart was restored. Once denying Jesus three times, Peter now professes his penance three times over; "I love you" "I love you" "I love you."

So how can we live a life like Peter, who through our inadequacies, imperfections, and failings, can shamelessly run into the waters of God's love? How can we stop keeping a long-running record of the ways in which we don't measure up? How can we transform those places of perfection-seeking for ourselves and for our children into spaces of stretching and blessing? And when we are tempted to self-rely, self-loathe, or self-condemn, how can we let the voice of Jesus whisper over us "I love you, I love you, I love you"? Maybe the voice of a mother who dove into the restoring waters of healing can shed light on letting go of perfectionism in motherhood. My dear and beloved friend, Beth Sri, knows all too well the imploding effect of believing the lie that our mistakes and transgressions define who we are. Loving mother of eight with a passion for sharing the Gospel with others, Beth has a deep love for Jesus and motherhood. It is my prayer that her gentle words will penetrate hearts so that mothers can find rest and renewal in the ocean of God's love. Speaking to the young-mom heart, Beth tenderly reminds us of God's unending love, a love that not only keeps no record of wrong, but who has the power to *forget*. "I, I am He who blots out your transgressions for my own sake, and *I will not remember your sins*" (Isaiah 43:25, emphasis added).

Love Does Not Keep a Record of Wrongs

BETH SRI

Dear Younger Me,

I see you … in the beautiful, chaotic phase of life with several little ones at home. I see you trying so hard to keep the house in order, giving yourself to your children, making a home that feels safe, calm, and cheerful. I see you … open to life, pregnant again, schlepping kids to Mass, to the store, to field trips. I see you … working so hard to stay on top of it all: planning meals, keeping the budget, coordinating the community All Saints Day party, wanting everything to be just right. I see you spending time with dear friends, with the college students, with extended family—trying so hard to please them all, all the time. I see you … Trying, working, providing, welcoming, showing up, giving, always giving.

And you're so tired, bone tired. How much does this vocation of marriage and motherhood take? It's exhilarating finally to be in the thick of the vocation to which Jesus has called you. At the same time, you've never felt more inadequate. You had been so used to doing it all, being it all ... and then, all of a sudden—boom! Where did that get-it-done, excellence-seeking, full-of-energy woman even go?

And I know what your knee-jerk tendency is when you feel that inadequacy: to try harder, do more, plan better, and anticipate the unexpected. Harder! Faster! Better! It's the mantra of Self-Reliance 101. You feel like you're drowning, and when you're sinking, it's natural to grasp at anything that seems like it might help. So, looking back, I understand why you worked so hard to be your own life raft, clinging to the familiar coping mechanism of self-reliance.

And that renewed commitment to doing things right, that willful forcing it to go better, starts to work a bit for you. Things begin to go the way you think they should, and you feel safe again ... for a time. Until the inevitable happens and a ball gets dropped: Dinner doesn't turn out great when the pastor comes over. You forget to bring treats for the soccer team when it's your family's turn, disappointing every child in attendance. Maybe you overspend on something that looks cute online but doesn't even fit because you still have the postpartum body shape. You snap at your husband and yell at the kids. Sometimes you just don't feel like praying, so you skip it and scroll on social media instead.

You find yourself right back in the same awful place as before, feeling inadequate, "less than," wrong, weak. And you feel powerless to change. Awash in shame, you ask: "Why is it easier for everyone else? Why am I not good enough to hack it? What's wrong with me?"

This shame you feel forms an unholy alliance with self-condemnation—those ugly thoughts that you beat yourself up with inside. "Why did I think that dress would fit?!" "Why didn't I look at the calendar before the game today—now everyone is disappointed and hungry because of me!" "*She* finds time to pray every single day." "What if everyone is starting to see that I don't have it all together?"

I see you, young Mama, so tired, feeling like there's no other way forward but to jump back into the vortex of ultra-planning, the uber control of self-reliance once again. "Maybe this time, if I

just try harder … maybe this time, I finally could be the mom I want to be instead of failing every day."

It's a wicked tornado: self-reliance feeding self-condemnation feeding yet another desperate grasp at self-reliance that only picks you up and takes you nowhere that you want to be: Nowhere near Jesus, nowhere near your husband and kids, nowhere near your friends and community. Yes, you are physically present to them all, but your mind and heart are always on the hamster wheel, striving to outrun your own deep-seated unworthiness, working with all your might to escape the impending avalanche of wrong and failure you fear is about to envelop everything.

And then you look at your darling children. I see your motherly heart and deep desire for them to know how much they are loved by you and how good they are in the eyes of God. You hope they will always have a deep and abiding knowledge of that love as the foundation for their lives. But one thing I wish became more visible earlier in life is how your own perfection-driven anxiety and shame was not just a problem for you—it was something that could keep your children from the secure love of our God who does not keep a record of wrongs (see 1 Corinthians 13:5).

I remember when I started to see the first hints of it: Seeing my son put pressure on himself to play the piano piece *exactly* right … and his harsh assessment of himself when he didn't perform it perfectly at the recital. Seeing my young daughter try *so* hard on a math test and her frustration at herself for not getting an

A. And then it hit me: they have it, too. The perfectionism and shame must have somehow seeped out of me … and began to touch my children. They must have sensed it within me and subconsciously pieced it together, picking up on my own lack of interior peace. Taking it into themselves by a sort of osmosis, the pressure I put on myself was starting to infiltrate the air they breathed.

**There is a way to find freedom
from the cycle of perfectionism and shame
and make a lasting change
for you and your darling children.**

How did this happen? The way that I saw myself, dear Mama, is the same lens through which I viewed my little ones. The harsh voice I used toward myself in my head was starting in subtle ways to creep into the way I sometimes engaged my children.

But sweet mama, the good news is there is a remedy. There is a way to find freedom from the cycle of perfectionism and shame and make a lasting change for you and your darling children.

The answer lies in the golden rule of love. Jesus said to love your neighbor as yourself. He didn't say love your neighbor *more* than yourself. He puts those two loves on an equal plane together. Love your neighbor. Love yourself. He links these two phases with a simple word: "as." From this connection, we can understand that the two will always be united; one will flow from the other. Simply put, *the way that we love ourselves is the way that we will love our neighbor.*

So, if I pressure myself to be perfect, I will end up disappointed when my kids are less than perfect. If I'm harsh in how I think about myself, my anxiety will taint the interactions I have with my children. If I compare myself to others and find myself lacking, I will be more likely to compare my kids to others and worry about their faults more than delight in the good qualities they possess. In sum, my interior view of myself becomes the default setting for how I show up for my neighbor.

So, the way you learn to truly love your children doesn't begin with them. It begins with you, in your own heart, in learning to love yourself in the way that God loves you. It's that simple and that difficult. The way of freedom from the shame—the pile of "less thans" and "not enoughs" that can sometimes swallow you up—is not to try harder, but to begin where you are. To accept that you are human and have limitations and weaknesses. To realize that God, who knows all your shortcomings, delights in you still. He is with you in your imperfections and desires to reveal his heart to you in those places of poverty. To accept that you *will* make mistakes is part of the process of growth and provides an invitation for you to turn toward Jesus and embrace just how much you need him.

God offers more guidance in learning to love this way, for 1 Corinthians 13:5 says, "Love does not keep a record of wrongs."[11]

The key in this verse is the phrase "does not *keep* a record." Wrongs and failures will always be a part of life. It's the holding on to our failures and imperfections that keep us buried in shame and blind to the gift Jesus offers. Accepting that you will fail and be wrong—yet still are loved—is the first step on the path to freedom.

Instead of keeping a record of your mistakes, failings, and inadequacies, you can approach them as stepping stones to discovering who you are as his daughter—beloved and cherished for who you are, not for what you accomplish and no matter how many failings you may have. As St. John Paul II said, "*We are not the sum of our weaknesses and failures; we are the sum of the Father's love for us.*"[12]

Indeed, the God who keeps no record of wrong sees past your shortcomings and gazes on the depths of your heart. His gentle and compassionate face invites you to an exchange, to look at him and see his love for you reflected in his gaze. St. John of the Cross describes the soul's gaze on God this way:

You looked with love upon me
and deep within your eyes imprinted grace
this mercy set me free ...
to lift my eyes adoring to your face.
–*Spiritual Canticle*, stanza 23, Iain Matthew translation

Delighting in you as you are, God longs to take that self-reliance and self-condemnation from your hands—through prayer, through Adoration, and especially through the beautiful Sacrament of Reconciliation. He longs to meet you in these encounters and release the burden of "not enough" and wrongdoing that keeps you bound.

And the more this becomes a regular practice for you, the more you will have a sixth sense whenever the ominous

Indeed, the God who keeps no record of wrong sees past your shortcomings and gazes on the depths of your heart.
His gentle and compassionate face invites you to an exchange, to look at him and see his love for you reflected in his gaze.

cloud of shame-bearing "record of wrongs" might move in to overshadow your dear children. You will see it in them, and you will be able to call it out with compassion. Free from the chains of your own shame, you will have capacity to hold them in their own. Your free, abiding love for them—flowing from your own deep experience of God's peaceful, unconditional love for you—will help make those "records of wrongs" that your children might be tempted to keep for themselves lessen or disappear. For your open, motherly embrace will radiate the face of God.

Instead of keeping records of wrongs—your own or your family's—you will learn to *keep* and hold on to something else. Our Lady "kept" and pondered the love of God in her heart. May you also hold fast to the *record of the mercies* of our Lord in your life, as well as his promises of a future full of hope (see Jeremiah 29:11)—for those are truly the only things worth keeping and holding on to.

In our Jesus,

BETH

– PRAYER –

*Sweet Jesus, thank you
for your endless love and mercy.
What did I do to earn
the compassion of the King of the World,
who delights in me, warts and all?
Please, Lord, give me the grace
to remember this as I move through
the exhausting days of my motherhood.
Help me to receive the hearts of my children anew every day,
rather than allowing the pains and sorrows
of the prior day to muddle my motherhood.
Please give me the grace to be patient
with the perceived inadequacies
in both my children and myself and help break the chains
of perfectionism from my heart.
Thank you for showing me what it means to love with abandon.
I love you.*

Amen.

Love Does Not Delight in Evil, but Rejoices in Truth

Where I found truth, there found I my God, the Truth itself.

ST. AUGUSTINE

The truth is that this thing called motherhood may be the hardest thing we will ever do. The sleepless nights, endless messes, toddler meltdowns, lack of alone time, and physical exhaustion that come from caring for the souls in our home can lead to secret daydreams of the seemingly easier days when we could choose when to eat, sleep, and work. We may idolize the days when we could carry on an uninterrupted conversation with a friend, go on a much-needed dinner date with our spouse, take the 'do nothing' tropical vacation we dream about, or simply spend time perusing shops for the latest outfit.

Maybe our daydreams are even simpler, maybe we just miss the days when we could choose to use the restroom without the chorus of banging little hands and feet hurrying up our three minutes of quietness. Perhaps, we remember with great delight the days when we ate our own lunch, rather than our children's crust or the last few bites of mac and cheese left in their bowls. Maybe we relish in the old days when long relaxing showers had a routine and a rhythm, rather than the hurried fit-it-in-to-clean-up-the-spit-up kind of shower many of us now find ourselves in.

The truth is motherhood is brutally hard. Truth is, every single mother that has ever walked this earth, would wholeheartedly agree, even if maybe she won't admit it. But somehow lost amongst the dishes and the diapers is the greater truth that motherhood is more majestic than it is difficult, more abounding than it is hard. The tiny hand that can clench around a pinky, the silly laughter and delight of goofy faces or outrageous dances, the exchange of love shared with each person whose tiny body once grew within our own, are incredible reflections of the Father's love, if we only slow down enough to recognize it.

Many of us have bought into the lie that hard equals bad. But sweet mommas, it's time to be gentle with ourselves. For it isn't our fault that we have lost sight of the truth. We have been duped by a culture that unequivocally shouts to the world the lie that children are a burden, a project, a duty, a task to be accomplished. We have been tricked into believing that *once my children are all grown and independent, then I will live life fully again*—or—*I must do everything I can to get my life back; hurry up and get them to bed.* The world constantly hammers the lie that independence and autonomy are the golden ticket. Yet the

beauty of marriage, children, and family life reveal the truth that we were divinely created for intimacy, connection, and communion, a communion that invites the soul to union with the Divine. For it is within the sanctuary of our homes that the sacred truth of God's love often births a life of love and sacrifice, joy and surrender. And how can we deny this magnificent truth, when Jesus himself says, "Whoever receives one such child in my name receives me" (Mark 9:37). Every cup of water we serve, every shirt we wash, every tear we wipe, and every heart we console are direct expressions of our love of Christ, who is Truth, himself.

Jesus says, "I am the way, and the *truth*, and the life" (John 14:6, emphasis added). Truth, period. No relative truth, no muddled truth, no *my* truth. Simply truth itself. Yet our culture handles the idea of objective truth with discomfort and distaste. Perhaps this is because hidden beneath this rejection of truth is a fear that it cannot be trusted, especially when the truth can be both hard and glorious.

This is precisely where the Pharisees found themselves. The carpenter from Nazareth just told the people, "I am the light of the world; he who follows me will not walk in darkness, but

will have the light of life" (John 8:12). They had just heard an answer to their desperate prayers. Yet the Pharisees, caught up with the legalities of the faith and a pride big enough to block their hearts from *knowing* God, looked at this man of mercy and love and decided he could not be trusted: "Your testimony is not true" (John 8:13). They said he was a fraud and that everything he said was a lie. But Jesus swiftly rebukes their suspicious hearts:

> *My testimony is true,*
> *for I know where I have come from*
> *and where I am going,*
> *but you do not know*
> *where I have come from*
> *or where I am going.*
> –John 8:14, emphasis added

Do we *know* where Christ came from? Do we know where he was going? Do we believe his own words: "I came from the Father and have come into the world; again, I am leaving the world and going to the Father" (John 16:28)? Do we believe that he offered himself on the Cross for us? Do we believe that he would do it all over again, if only just for *me*, for *you*? Do we believe in his Divinity and his tender care? Or does the fear of hard things leave our distrusting hearts crying out, "Your testimony is not true!"

Lucky for us, my friends, this is not where Christ's truth ends. No, he goes on to say, "I have said this to you, that in me you may have *peace*. In the world you have tribulation; but be of good cheer, I have overcome the world" (John 16:33, emphasis added). He doesn't promise that motherhood will be easy, that the house will stay clean, or that we can avoid the many nights of heavy tears our maternal hearts will experience. But he does promise the greater peace and joy of his divine love and care, which the banquet of family life allows us to feast on. Our days may be hard, but they are beautiful, even when they may not feel that way. The hardness does not negate the gift. The *Catechism of the Catholic Church* highlights the truth of this dichotomy: "The Catholic wisdom of the people is capable of fashioning a vital synthesis … that radically affirms the dignity of every person as a child of God, establishes a basic fraternity, teaches people to encounter nature and understand work, provides reasons for joy and humor even in the midst of a very hard life" (CCC 1676).

Yes, truth is, motherhood is back-breakingly hard. But truth is it is also heart-expanding, soul-stretching, and life-givingly good.

Yes, truth is, motherhood is back-breakingly hard. But truth is it is also heart-expanding, soul-stretching, and life-givingly good. Only God could have fashioned the heart of a mother to be such an exquisite vessel of love to hold the heavy and the light, the hope and the trembling, the joy and the sorrow. With a love that quite literally feels like it will explode from within the depths of the maternal heart, motherhood gives us a glorious foretaste of the splendor of God's love.

How can we rest in the truth of the divine goodness of our maternal vocations? How can we crush the lie that children are a burden? How can we trust that this family life, which God has carefully crafted for us, is the most perfect place to sip on the cup of his love, here and now? Perhaps, a mother who has labored through the hard and exhausting and has found herself birthing a love of beauty and joy can breathe life into the young-mom heart. Homeschooling mom of nine, my cherished friend, Carrie Daunt, has an intense love for her Heavenly Father and a passion for healing and restoring the beauty of family life. It is my prayer that her tender words can be a source of raw encouragement for the weary heart. I hope that, through her letter, the Holy Spirit will crush our fear of the hard and cement our hearts with the life-giving truth of the good.

Love Does Not Delight in Evil, but Rejoices in Truth

CARRIE DAUNT

Dear Younger Self,

You gave birth to your ninth baby this year. Twenty-two years and two days after the first. You cried all the way to the hospital to deliver him. Heavy, hot tears spilled down your cheeks as a slideshow of the last two decades of memories ran through your mind. It was not a grief over having a baby. It was the grief of knowing that this precious baby would rip your heart wide open with love. And that one day, you would have to learn to let him go.

You see, when you had your eighth baby, the landscape of life looked very different. You were still in your thirties and all your kids were living under one roof. While the years with a house full of little ones were often chaotic and crazy, every night you could rest easy knowing they were all right down the hall, tucked into their beds. The seven years spanning the birth of your eighth and ninth children became a season of letting go. First, it was the license to drive. Watching your daughter pull out of the driveway the first day she drove to school was your initial taste of learning to surrender. A few years later, when she decided on college several states away, your heart felt like it was packing up and moving with her. As you drove away after dropping her off, you felt like you were leaving a part of yourself there. You knew this day would one day arrive, yet you were blindsided with grief the first night you walked down the hall to say goodnight to her, and she was no longer sleeping in her bed.

Two years later, you dropped off our oldest son in the same state as his sister and left with the same hole. When he left for college, he was profoundly missed. His siblings lost their fearless leader, the captain of fun. For months, the younger kids would end every day saying, "I wish Drew were still here."

He was missed so much that when your third child, Ryan, was discerning college the very next year, he almost gave up his appointment to a military academy to follow his older brother to his college. After much prayer, tears, and discernment, he ended up in Colorado at the Air Force Academy. It was the hardest goodbye. You had to drop him off and drive off. No farewell. No hug. No lingering. Dozens of screaming cadres were his welcome to boot camp. You had no contact with him for weeks. This was a new kind of loss and a greater letting go.

With two more in high school and three others trailing right behind them, you realize this is just the beginning of a long stream of goodbyes. If anyone had told you this stage would be harder than having these babies back-to-back, you would have never believed them.

Your early years of motherhood were entirely consuming. You spent every minute of every day nurturing, caring, providing, and protecting them. You loved each one of these children with your entire being and gave them everything you had. This poverty of your time and freedom was a constant offering. An offering that grew with each child you welcomed. Each child was such a unique gift. Each child revealed to you another facet of God the Father's love. Each child changed the dynamic of your family forever and for good.

During those years, it also became clear that most of the world did not see things the same way. Most of the culture bought into the insidious lie that children are a burden and not a gift. Having a big family was not only counter-cultural but also often opposed. Nearly every time you had the courage to venture out with all your kids, the man at the grocery store or the woman at Mass would tell you that you were crazy and in over your head. Your own pediatrician mocked you for having so many kids. To compound things, some of your Catholic family would talk about your careless family planning behind your back, and closest friends would exclude you from social gatherings because you had too many kids in tow.

Yet despite the adversity and judgment (and never having a free moment to go to the bathroom), you can now see those years were the most intimate, content, and joyful years of your life. While it was a hard season marked with many sacrifices, out of this season, so much life was cultivated inside of your home.

Over the last seven years, you have come to embrace these precious wonder years of childhood. You learned to savor the gift. The whole world paints the picture of kids growing up and leaving the nest as the most natural thing on earth. You hear stories about the vacations empty nesters take, the money they save, and the time they have to themselves, while you simply cannot understand how to turn off the ache of every goodbye. Learning to let go feels as unnatural as trying to suck toothpaste back into the tube. You wonder, do all those years of maternal instinct magically turn off the instant they leave home?

Eventually, the depth of the ache lessens. You begin seeing flashes of your child becoming who they are. These moments are beautiful consolations. You often think of Jesus in the Temple teaching while Mary is frantically searching for him in the caravan. While Jesus feels lost to his mother, Jesus knows exactly where he is and what he is to do. He is entering his Father's mission. Like Jesus, these moments are your child's invitation to begin the mission God has for their life and to multiply the gift. Venturing out on their own is both good and necessary.

> **Like Jesus, these moments are your child's invitation to begin the mission God has for their life and to multiply the gift.**

The time you have with your kids when they are all under your roof is precious time. One day they will no longer need you to change their explosive diaper, tie their muddy shoe, or help them with their dreaded homework. Those dog-tired early years when everyone was in hugging distance will be remembered as the good old days. The next season will come quicker than you think, and you will give anything to have all your kids with you at the grocery store or at Mass. You would welcome the unkind comments, all for the chance to witness to the gift of life and togetherness. In God's goodness, the ninth child you received in the twilight of your childbearing years offered you the opportunity to relive all those precious moments again with a brand-new perspective.

After his delivery, you found yourself sobbing for the second time that day. Tears of joy and surrender. You will go through all of this again. You will love this baby with all of your being. It is worth every second and sacrifice. Your fervent yes to all that motherhood has to offer is a testimony to truth. You will not let a world that delights in evil steal one second of your joy. You will rejoice in the truth. No matter how they get here, when they come, or how far they go, children are always a gift.

Savor every moment!

With Love,
YOUR OLDER SELF

- PRAYER -

*My Jesus, thank you for crafting the family
to be a magnificent expression of your love.
You have beautifully fashioned mother and child
to be an intricately connected experience of the Divine.
When the world begins to impress the lies of burden
upon my heart, please fix my eyes upon you
so I can be steadfast in your perfect truths;
the truth of abounding goodness, deep intimacy, connection,
and communion. Let my heart be filled with a
treasuring awareness of the wild gift of the little souls
I have the honor of loving. I pray that when the days
get difficult, exhausting, and back-breakingly hard,
I will remember that it is all worth it.
The price of sleepless nights, sticky floors, aches and pains, and
every broken item we once cherished,
are wildly worth the immeasurable prize of this
beautiful thing called family life.*

Amen.

Love Bears All Things

Honor, revere, and respect the Blessed Virgin Mary with a particular love. She is the mother of our sovereign Lord, and therefore we are her children. Thus, let us turn to her and, as her little children, let us cast ourselves into her embrace with full confidence; at all times and places let us call upon this sweet mother, invoking her maternal love, and let us strive to imitate her virtues, with a truly filial love for her in our hearts.

ST. FRANCIS DE SALES

Merriam Webster Dictionary defines "to bear" as "to hold, to support, to accept." We mommas are generally really good at holding and supporting all things for the sake of our loved ones. We hold the infant on our backs, the laundry in our arms, and the weight of their hearts in our souls. We support their little necks and their biggest dreams. We hold their tiny hands as they learn to shuffle one foot in front of the other. But accept? This is something entirely different. There is no doubt that we accept the giggles, the kisses, and the snuggles. We may even accept the interrupted sleep, the muddy feet, and the never-ending messes. But to accept all things? It may not be as easy to bear when they struggle to read, don't make the team, or collapse under the weight of their own pain and suffering.

But before we get too hard on ourselves, let's understand that it makes sense that we struggle to endure the suffering of those we love. You see, we mommas were created with a distinctive protective instinct that has awarded many of us the title of "Mama Bear." Originating from mother bears who are known to be fiercely protective of their cubs and aggressive toward any sensed threat, *Mama Bear* sheds light on the rescuing heart of a mother. By studying animals, scientists have discovered that

this protective instinct is associated with the hormone oxytocin, which is released during childbirth and breastfeeding.[13] We mothers were quite literally designed to risk our lives to protect those of our children. But what if real protection, the eternal kind of protection, doesn't always mean eliminating the harm that will come their way? What if it means being willing to bear with them, behind them, and beside them, to the point of death, and perhaps *even after*?

One quiet and hidden character in biblical history shows us that even death cannot stop a mother from bearing the suffering of her child. Two of the late King Saul's sons, Armoni and Mephibosheth, were handed over to the Gibeonites as a sacrifice, put to death, and brutally left discarded and exposed upon a hill. The story of these two men could simply be one of violence and discardment. Yet, the ugly nature of this story is interrupted by the protective and bearing love of a mother in mourning. "Then Rizpah the daughter of Aiah took sackcloth, and spread it for herself on the rock, from the beginning of harvest until rain fell upon them from the heavens; and she did not allow the birds of the air to come upon them by day, or the beasts of the field by night" (2 Samuel 21:10). She laid down her body, her life, quite literally to protect the bodies of the children she once nursed, once clothed, once held. She bore in their suffering right there on the makeshift graveyard on a hill. She bore her own body to cover their lifeless ones from being dishonored.

Throughout Scripture, God continuously reveals the profound and protective love of a mother. He even places our hearts into the hands of his own mother when from the Cross he says, "Behold, your mother!" (John 19:27). He quietly whispers, *If you want to love me, then let my Mother mother you!* It may feel counter-intuitive to think we should go to someone else to love God more deeply. And yet, Christ is persistent. He leads us into the arms of Mary. To cement this truth into my own heart, he continuously illuminates the same image over and over again in my mind:

I'm three or four years old, standing in an open field. The tall grass sways in the wind while the sun shines so bright I can barely open my eyes. Ahead of me, I see the most gorgeous wildflowers, and yet I'm afraid. I am terrified of my limitedness, my littleness. How can I care for these most precious and beautiful flowers? It is too much for my tiny hands! But then I feel a gentle squeeze of my hand, the reassuring kind of squeeze. I look up and see that attached to this hand is the arm of the most beautiful woman. I gaze upward and see her hair blowing in the wind, yet somehow, I cannot see her face. She stands forward next to me, calm, confident, and strong. With her warming presence, I feel secure. I feel safe. I feel protected. She holds, she supports, she accepts. She bears. So like a timid toddler with mother, I clench her leg and hide behind her swaying summer dress, and with my hand in hers, she slowly walks me into the awaiting field of flowers. In this moment, and within her embrace, I can do anything.

Into this maternal heart is where God leads me, leads all of us, for she can only lead us more confidently back to him. The *Catechism of the Catholic Church* says it best: "From the most ancient times the Blessed Virgin has been honored with the title of 'Mother of God,' to whose *protection* the faithful fly in all their dangers and needs" (CCC 971, emphasis added). In the safety of a mother who will fight the dragons, stomp the serpent's head, and tend the flowers in the field, all while radiating peace, beauty, and joy.

So how can Mary's love teach us to *bear all things* for the little hearts and souls we love? When our children have to walk into the lion's den of new experiences, face the burning home of heartache, or leap over the precipices of the unknown, how can our maternal hearts be willing to bear the cross with them? And when our feeble hands are unable to save them from all the wounds of this world, how can we trust that there is a God who will never stop rescuing them? This is where my sweet friend Laura Phelps comes in. A mother of four with a fiery devotion to Momma Mary, Laura has lain down at the foot of the Cross with maternal heartache and pain. But through the tender embrace of Mary, Laura has tasted the sweetness of the Cross and has found herself standing once again. Through her gentle words to the young mom's heart, I pray that we can let go of our ungodly self-reliance and rest in knowing we were never called to fix it all, but rather to *bear it all* with our maternal love, a surrendered kind of love.

Love Bears All Things

LAURA PHELPS

Hey, Super Mom!

If I buy you a latte, could you get off that gerbil wheel of production and hear what I have to say? Don't worry; I'm not here to judge your earlier years of mothering. I'm not even going to warn you about how much you're going to mess up your kids. (Just kidding. You only mess them up a little.) I know what being a Mother means to you. It's everything. Falling short of perfection in all that you do is not an option. *Mother* is not only what you believe you do but also who you believe you are. And so, trust me, I get it. I get you. And I am not here to criticize. I'm here to say *I see you*. I know the fear that drives you. And if I could go back in time, I would get down on the floor next to you, hand you a latte (non-fat, of course), and whisper the words you so needed to hear but nobody said:

It's not all up to you.

From the moment of conception, you bought into the lie that Mother was your identity and your children's well-being would directly reflect how well you loved. And you are not entirely wrong. Of course, your love matters! Love is what moves you—literally. It moves you out of the comfort of your bed at 2 am to console a teething baby, out of your plans to pick up a sick child from school 30 minutes after you dropped her off. It's even moved you up a pant size. Motherhood dug a new well of love in your heart, and dare I say, that love produced the best goodie bags and cakes a kid could hope for. If children's birthday parties were a contest, you, my dear, would have won.

It's a vocation—a calling. God loves you
and calls you to Motherhood.
Not based on what you do,
but on *whose* you are.

But motherhood isn't a contest.

It's a vocation—a calling. God loves you and calls you to Motherhood. Not based on what you do, but on *whose* you are. You've forgotten (or perhaps you never knew) that before you became *Mother*, you were *daughter*. That's right. You were *daughter* first, my dear. The daughter of a mighty King who formed you, knew you (see Jeremiah 1:5), and planted within you the heart of a mother. Motherhood is not a trophy to achieve but a gift to receive.

You didn't have to fill out an application or interview. It was given to you by God.

This means that you have nothing to prove.

You don't have to be the best at everything to earn your keep. You don't have to put yourself last to show how much you sacrifice. You don't have to put your kids in matching pajamas on Christmas Eve...or ever, for that matter, to be a great mom.

You don't even have to bathe your kids every night because, honestly, that nighttime routine is killing you, and dirty kids grow up just fine. Remember the girl from kindergarten class who showed up to your birthday party wearing an outfit that clearly needed to go through the wash? She went on to become the valedictorian of an Ivy League school. True story. All I'm saying is that a bit of dirt is not the worst thing, and skipping a night is okay. Read the book, tuck them in, and pour the wine because you are exhausting me.

Here's the thing: how well you love your kids is not measured by how perfectly things turn out, how happy they are, or how enchanting your life looks on Instagram. Children are not a project. They are people. And people have free will. Mistakes,

destructive choices, and tragedies happen despite how hard you try to avoid them. Your love has nothing to do with how well you do it all. Get that lie out of your head because here is the truth, and you might want to add a shot of Bailey's or something to your coffee before I continue …

Your love, fierce and strong as it may be, is not enough to shield your children from suffering. You can micro-manage all you want when they are too little to have an opinion and small enough to swaddle or strap down. But try strapping your one-day teenage daughter in a chair or wrapping your young adult son so tight in a blanket that he can't move (Don't actually do this. You'll get arrested.) Have you heard the term "helicopter parent"? Don't get excited; it's not a compliment, and from how you manage your tiny crew, helicoptering is where you are heading. I know what you are thinking. *"I'm not overprotective! I am doing what any good mother who loves her children does."* And that's not entirely untrue. But I've got years on you, so I see better. (With the help of bifocals, I see better.) Yes, it is about love. But a mother's love doesn't shield her children from suffering. A mother's love *shares* in her children's suffering.

I know. You don't want to share in their suffering; you want to remove it. You want to jump into action, heal the pain, and cover the wound. And the thing is, when they are little, sometimes you can. Never underestimate the power of a Scooby Doo Band-Aid and chocolate Tootsie Pop. But it's short-lived. Before you know it, a child's pain becomes too much—even for a mother's love, and we are forced to accept our new role. But do we? After all, what mother allows pain? What mother stands and watches her child suffer?

Do you remember that Sunday morning when you couldn't find your son? Mass had ended, and while chatting with friends, your four-year-old ran off. Minutes (that felt like hours) later, you found him outside the church, kneeling before the statue of Our Blessed Mother. You marveled at this precious sight but didn't grasp the full magnitude of that sacred moment. Our Lady was calling you to her, not only directing you where you should go in moments of panic, fear, and chaos but also giving you the sweet assurance that when separated from your children, she would be with them.

What mother stands and watches her child suffer, you ask?

Your Heavenly Mother, that's who. And with her help, so you will, too.

I've frightened you, haven't I? The thought of something terrible happening to your children terrifies you, doesn't it? You could never stand by and watch. You'd buckle down and set to work. Lose a child? Not on your watch. That's why when suffering threatens to intersect with your children's lives, you look for their way out. The problem with this is that the Cross has no escape door. And oh, how you will waste years searching for it! If I could go back and tell you one thing, it would be this:

You cannot remove your child's cross. But like Mary, you can help bear it.

1 Corinthians 13:7: *Love bears all things*. The Greek word for bear is *stego*, which means to cover and protect. But protecting is not the same as preventing. A roof will protect us from getting soaked, but it will not prevent us from experiencing the storm. Your job is not to stop the storm but to endure it. Notice that St. Paul doesn't say love *fixes* all things; he says love *bears* all things. Other definitions of the word "bears" are supports, abides, and stands. In short—and I know it sounds crazy—*love lets the ones we most love fall.*

You don't believe me?

Look at Mary, who watched her beloved Son fall three times on the way to Calvary. She did not try to prevent it from happening. She did not carry the Cross for him. But her love bore it all. Learn from her example. I know that this is not easy on your mama's heart. This is why I beg you to stay close to Our Lady. Her heart knows your pain—she understands how a mother's heart mirrors the heart of her child. In the days you can't bear the pain any longer, trade your super cape for her mantle and let yourself be daughter.

I should let you go now, but I have one last thing to say. Like your Mama Mary, you are a Warrior, and I am so proud of you. The enemy is going to tempt you into believing that you're a failure. Nothing could be further from the truth. Rebuke that lie and throw it in the pit of hell where it belongs because your *best love* will be *the hardest love* and spoiler alert: *you will survive*. Remember, this story—yours and your child's—is far from over. The ink is still wet, and the pen is in God's hands, not yours. So finish your latte, get back to your kids, and as torturous as it feels, play one more game of Chutes and Ladders because one day, you will miss it. But above all else, never forget that a mother's love is not about "crushing it." It's about not letting the trials of life crush you; it's about persevering in the pain, sharing in the suffering, and standing when we are most tempted to run.

With so much love,

FUTURE, STRONGER, *STANDING* YOU

- PRAYER -

*Jesus, thank you for
always carrying, supporting, and
accepting me, your beloved.
I am grateful for the protective instinct
that you have infused into my maternal heart.
Please give me the grace to
destroy the lie that motherhood requires
repairing or preventing all the pain and sorrow
that my child will experience.
Instead, give me the heart to hold,
support, and bear their suffering along with them.
Please give me the docility to open my heart
to the maternal love of your most perfect mother, Mary.
Allow me to become little before her so
that she may scoop me up her in arms
and mantle giving me the courage to
maternally bear all things.*

Amen.

Love Believes All Things

A humble soul does not trust itself,
but places all its confidence in God.

ST. FAUSTINA

I often believe that I trust God with every ounce of my being. I have walked, or better yet stumbled my way through many hardships in this life where, with tears of grief and sorrow, I have surrendered it all into God's hands; the fracturing of a family, the suicide of a loved one, the abandonment of friends, the uprooting of a community, and once the threat that this mother of six was going to be wheelchair-bound as a result of a potential diagnosis. Yet, I have begun to notice that I can believe in God's good promises with the big things of the past or future, while the crumbling anxiety of the small, here-and-now, things of my life are usually suffocated within the grip of my fear and control. Our Lord calls us to trust him in all things, especially the here and now. He tells us, "Do not be anxious about tomorrow" (Matthew 6:34).

Do I believe God's promises with the mess in my home? Do I trust God and his abiding presence when the baby

screams, the dinner is burnt, or my children's growing characters seem to be going awry? I once heard that if God had a love language it would likely be "trust." Boom and yikes. I desire to give God the love he deserves by fully trusting him with the big *and* small. Yet, I'll be honest, my friends. The fear and anxiety of the lonely heart of a child, the delayed reading schedule of another, or the sudden onset of lying from little hearts can spiral this mom's heart through a tornado of future projection that it robs me of the quiet surrender and trust in the here and now. I may be able to trust God with *my* life, but can I trust enough to surrender *their* lives to him? I have found myself praying about what it means and looks like to respond to God and his call on my motherhood and my life in the small things and present, and not merely on the big things and past.

"Here I am" are three small words that have been reverberating in my heart for some time now. It's a heart cry that came out of the mouth of Abraham when the Lord called to him. Not knowing that God was about to ask him to sacrifice his only miraculous son Isaac, Abraham swiftly responded with, "Here I am." The Hebrew word for this phrase, *Hineni*, used only a few times throughout Scripture, is an intimate and powerful response implying an open heart totally willing to act.

I once heard that if God
had a love language
it would likely be "trust."

Following God's command to sacrifice Isaac, with a total willingness to be obedient to whatever God asks, Abraham immediately arises the next morning to carry out God's request of him. "Abraham put forth his hand, and took the knife to slay his son. But the angel of the Lord called to him from heaven, and said, 'Abraham, Abraham!'" (Genesis 22:10–11). Abraham once again replied, *Hineni*! The Lord stopped Abraham from taking the life of his son for God's sake, but it wasn't but a mere moment before the sacrifice was to take place. Abraham simply believed. Simply trusted. Simply cried out, "Here I am."

God tells us, "For I, the Lord your God, hold your right hand; it is I who say to you, 'Fear not, I will help you'" (Isaiah 41:13). I want to believe he will help me, in fact, I need to. The *Catechism of the Catholic Church* says that "'to believe' has thus a twofold reference: to the person and to the truth; to the truth, by trust in the person who bears witness to it" (CCC 177).

Do I trust and believe in the person of God and the truth he says? Can I believe like Abraham? Can the heart cry of my life declare a loud *Hineni* to the heavens? Can my heart respond with a *Hineni* with every lonely tear I wipe or aching heart I console? Can I cry out *Hineni* when the baby wakes in the night, or when I forget to bake the banana bread for the women's coffee hour? Can I whisper *Hineni* with a belief so big that I can say it in the face of fear or, like Abraham, to the point of death?

Maybe a woman whose motherhood once had her locked behind the bars of fear can help show us the way of *Hineni*. With a heart that has slowly learned the little way of love and motherhood, Christine Hanus gives us a peek into what it means to lay down our motherhood with abiding belief and trust. Mother of five and a ferocious lover of God, Christine's honest words

encourage us to guard our hearts from the enemy and to trust in God's goodness. I pray that Christine's words will help us respond to Christ's invitation to a "filial trust in the providence of our heavenly Father" (CCC 322).

Love Believes All Things

CHRISTINE HANUS

Dear Younger Self,

Before I broach the topic of "trust," I just want to say that I saw this quote the other day and thought of you: *Talk to yourself as though you were someone you love.*

As you examine yourself in the mirror today, my friend, I urge you to talk to yourself with compassion, affection, and understanding. I'm glad you see your faults and failings so clearly, but remember, the Father loves you unconditionally. Plus, one of the dangers of being too hard on yourself is that you tend to become too hard on other people. No one needs that!

So … you recently had your third baby! Three boys now, all under the age of four. How cool and how crazy is that? Living in New Mexico, so far away from family and the support they can provide, makes it particularly challenging, but I know how much you love being a wife and mom. I remember this time well and so fondly.

Your boys are thrilled to have a new baby to "love up" as they like to say. Thankfully, that baby, almost nine pounds at birth, seems to thrive under their little-boy affection.

Though this new baby brings you indescribable joy, reality has set in. You are no longer a novice mom. Along with the exhilaration of each new little one, your idealism about family life has taken a hit. You certainly never expected to have so many concerns constantly weighing on your mind.

This week alone you have come face-to-face with a number of gut-punching "little" things: the fear that Baby's cold might

cause him to stop breathing in the night, that the toddler's desire to sleep naked signifies an aberration in his psyche, and that the deer mice, which have been happily eating all the peanut butter off the mousetraps in your home, will infect your children with the hantavirus. It can sound silly, but I know each of these fears cause you real anxiety and sometimes even panic.

Add to these concerns the state of the world around you. Partial-birth abortion, euthanasia, and cloning are becoming increasingly acceptable, and the fallout from broken families is ever more apparent. It is hard to picture your beloved children thriving in this wounded world.

But Jesus never promised this life would be easy. As a matter of fact, he said to his apostles, "In the world you will have trouble, but take courage, I have overcome the world."

As a follower of Christ from the time you were in fifth grade, you have been aware that we are "strangers and sojourners" in this life. This belief has enabled you to stay detached in some ways from the cares of the world. You have tried to value that which has eternal significance and to do your bit to make the world a better place.

But your awareness that you will never be permanently happy and fulfilled in this life has also taken its toll on you. You were unable to hide from the harsher realities of life. Your heart breaks with concern for the salvation and well-being of others. As a young person, you were persecuted for your faith, struggling with your temptations and weaknesses while your peers often seemed to be carefree.

Nevertheless, the prospect of persecution, danger, and alienation never paralyzed you. When you married Patrick, also a believer, you were fortified as you faced the world together with zeal and passion.

Then you received the gift of a child, which brings with it a new way of looking at the world, your life, and your God. Your fierce mother-love makes you feel less intrepid, less "in-control," less able to resist the temptation to fear. You wrote these words in your journal last week, "Another area in my spiritual life that troubles me greatly is my fear; my lack of trust. I feel so vulnerable since I have become a mother. I think of all the horrible things the Lord could allow to happen, and I recoil with fear—I am gripped by terror. I know and believe suffering can be redemptive, but … how does one bear it?"

Confidence in God
is at the root of every virtue,
every happiness.

Twenty-five years later, I cannot give you the answer to this question. Learning to accept the hardships and even the excruciatingly painful things in life is a process. A process that I am still undergoing. There is no magic formula that takes away your fear. There is no pill you can swallow to ease the anxiety at its root. There is no word that can be spoken that will give you enough light, so that you never fear the shadows and the scary dark corners of your mind.

But let me remind you of the things you already know and must continue to practice if you want to grow in trust of the Lord and experience joy and freedom in your motherhood.

First, recall how the enemy works and keep a diligent guard over your mind. "Resist the devil and he will flee from you. Draw near to God and he will draw near to you" (James 4:7–8). This mental and spiritual "exercise" requires effort, but this diligence is effective, building the kind of "muscle" we need in order to stay the course when the worst happens. And this radical trust is not just for times of darkness. Confidence in God is at the root of every virtue, every happiness. In particular, I think you need to take more control over the way that you use your imagination.

Think about your cross-country trip this summer and your tornado phobia. Now that you are back in New Mexico after a much-needed summer vacation with your extended family, perhaps the panic you experienced during the trip has faded … but cast your mind back. This example can serve as an analogy for all your fears and the role your imagination plays in feeding those fears.

Driving with three children under the age of four, side-by-side in the back seat of a small sedan, you and Patrick made your way through Tornado Alley as you do every summer. (Though I can smile about your fear of tornados now, I remember the barely controlled terror you were in as you drove through Oklahoma on that humid and stormy day.)

As with the other dangers you anticipate as a mother, the danger of tornados is not "all in your head." There is a real possibility that you may have to deal with a tornado in Oklahoma during the summer months. This summer, on the first leg of the journey, you had already been traveling for twelve hours—an eternity in toddler years—as you approached Oklahoma City. For some time, you had been racing just ahead of the storm, but at this point, you could clearly observe the ominous, gray clouds, arranged neatly above you like so many dark dinner rolls; Patrick knowledgeably called them "super cells," and he kept glancing at the sky saying comforting things like "Wow!" With a film of sweat on your upper lip, you prayed your family into relative safety in Iowa.

The thing is, you have an excellent imagination and, even though a tornado did not strike, you sat in the passenger seat and imagined one on the horizon; you imagined the frantic attempt to get three children out of their respective car seats and safely into a non-existent ditch. You let fear overtake you.

Mom, use the gift of your imagination differently. There are troubles and hard times that you cannot avoid in this life. They

will come, just as tornados will come to tornado alley every summer, but as soon as you notice that your imagination is running wild, picture Jesus in the moment. Put him into the scene. You and your husband only have four hands between you, but Jesus comes with a host of angels, and whatever your family must face, he is there. Maybe he will miraculously protect you. If not, he will give you the supernatural grace you need. In the words of St. Francis de Sales, "Do not fear what may happen tomorrow. The same loving Father who cares for you today will care for you tomorrow and every day. Either he will shield you from suffering, or he will give you unfailing strength to bear

it. Be at peace, then, and put aside all anxious thoughts and imaginings."

Along these same lines, I think you would find it helpful to explore Ignatian spirituality, particularly the concept of consolation and desolation. Consolations are moments when we feel sure of God's love and goodness and want to respond to him. Learn how to accept the consolations with gratitude and enjoy them! Desolations are from the enemy and lead you to lose hope—to believe the lie that you are not the Father's beloved child, and that God cannot be trusted. Learn how to resist desolations, not just passively accept them. Remember God's goodness to you and thank and praise him often. Use the words of Scripture as a sword to fight the battles in your mind and heart. This is what our beloved Jesus did in the desert, and this is how we, too, defeat Satan.

Ultimately, dear Younger Self, you will undergo some of the trials you fear. Other trials will pass you by. Just keep being as faithful as you can be today and lean into Jesus. Lean into Love.

Which brings me to my final point. You cannot and will not ever really trust the Lord if you do not know Jesus personally. You cannot know Jesus personally if you do not spend time with him, especially meditating on the Gospels. I know time is a valuable commodity just now, but nothing can take the place of intimacy with Christ, so take the time to be with Jesus every day in prayer, even if it can only be for ten minutes. Then continue your conversation with God throughout the day.

> You cannot and will not ever really trust the Lord if you do not know Jesus personally.

When you don't feel close to our Lord and perhaps even feel abandoned by him, say what is true and do what is right. Let your mantra be "Jesus, I trust in You," even if it must be said through gritted teeth, through tears of anguish, or in a broken monotone. Everything is going to be okay as long as you stay with Jesus. Believe me, he will stay with you! Ahhh, dear friend, the stories I could tell about his faithfulness. This life has been a grand adventure of love!

I will leave you with some words from St. Thérèse of Lisieux: "It is confidence and nothing but confidence which will lead us to love."[14] Relish the journey, Younger Self, guard your heart and mind, and persevere.

Love on!

YOUR OLDER SELF

- PRAYER -

*Heavenly Father, thank you
for holding me in the palm of your hand.
There is not a hair on my head
that falls without your permission.
There is no detail too small
for your tender care.
Please give me the grace
to trust you with the big and small,
hard and easy, messy and beautiful of my life.
I desire to entrust my life,
and the lives of my children to you.
Please help me to release the grip of worry,
and to "rise, and have no fear" (Matthew 17:7).
But if my fear begins to take my gaze off of you,
please rescue me like Peter
from the waters of anxiety and place me back
onto the shores of childlike trust.*

Amen.

Love Hopes All Things

Do not lose heart, even if you should discover that you lack qualities necessary for the work to which you are called. He who called you will not desert you, but the moment you are in need he will stretch out his saving hand.

ST. ANGELA MERICI

"They that *hope* in the Lord will renew their strength, they will soar on eagles' wings; they will run and not grow weary, walk and not grow faint" (Isaiah 40:31 NAB, emphasis added). I am not sure about you, but I could surely use a renewal of my strength. This achy, tired, and disheveled woman frequently moves through the day feeling as if she just finished running a marathon. But instead, it is through the daily grind of my vocation as a momma that my body, mind, and soul frequently grow weary. I worry, I fret, and I swell up with anxiety when I realize all the balls I once placed strategically in the air are not only crashing down but also bouncing all over the messy house. "I wasn't meant for this job," I'm tempted to pray. "God, you have the wrong girl. I'm simply not good enough." But *you are*, he says. I have chosen *you*, and

All of our fractured, messy, and exhausted stories are being redeemed with God!

ordained you, for this job, for *these* children. Yet I find myself, like Sarah in her old age, doubting God's promises.

But how can I laugh with doubt? I love God. I spend countless moments throughout the day in secret and life-giving conversations with him. He, along with Momma Mary, is the accompaniment to this beautifully messy life I now lead. He knows my dreams, my sorrows, my fears, my joys. I may be able to stand on a mountaintop and proclaim his goodness and promises of salvation for others, but where is my hope in the King of the World if I can only chuckle with doubt what he promises *me*? Paul tells us that "faith is the assurance of things *hoped* for, the conviction of things not seen" (Hebrews 11:1, emphasis added). Gulp, there it is, my friends. Without hope, our faith is dead.

The *Catechism of the Catholic Church* shares a little treasure with us, "Nothing is more apt to **confirm** our *faith* and *hope* than holding it fixed in our minds that nothing is impossible with God" (CCC 274, emphasis added). This is where the secret lies. Philippians 4:13, the first Bible passage my children and I ever memorized together, is the key to the sustaining faith and hope we need: "I can do all things in him who strengthens me." **Nothing** is impossible with God. Not *some things*, or *a majority of* things, but *nothing*!

Your motherhood, your marriage, your heart, your love, even the bouncing balls creating chaos around your home, **nothing** is impossible with God. All of our fractured, messy, and exhausted

stories are being redeemed with God! Pope Benedict XVI tells us that "Redemption is offered to us in the sense that we have been given *hope, trustworthy hope*, by virtue of which we can face our present: the present, even if it is arduous, can be lived and accepted if it leads towards a goal, if we can be sure of this goal, and if this goal is great enough to justify the effort of the journey."[15]

When we open ourselves up to receive this hope for which we have been given and trust that God can make life out of the ashes of our days, we will be able to come alive with the renewal of strength he promises.

Does our goal to love our children well and shepherd them toward a life spent in eternity with us glorifying our loving God justify the sleepless nights, the dirty floors, the tear-filled meltdowns, and the wear and tear on our bodies? The answer is YES. When we open ourselves up to receive this hope for which we have been given and trust that God can make life out of the ashes of our days, we will be able to come alive with the renewal of strength he promises. As our disbelief turns into hopeful waiting for all that he promises in *his* timing and in *his* way, we may even soar on wings like eagles. Or better yet, we may find ourselves laughing alongside Sarah, with jubilation this time because she "received power to conceive, even when she was past the age, since she considered him faithful who had promised" (Hebrews 11:11).

So how do we live out this Hope in God and his promises? It begins with believing that even in the hard and in the dark, he is working all things out for our good, *always*. Perhaps a mother who once found herself weary in her motherhood can help restore our hearts with the conviction of the eternal value of our vocation. Convert from Judaism and mother of four, my friend Debbie Herbeck pours her heart into helping women know the personal love of Jesus. It is my hope that her own personal experience of moving into hope and walking with Jesus in her motherhood can help reignite the heart of the weary mother. I pray her words will help to cement the virtue of Hope as a cornerstone of our maternal beings, giving us the strength to run and not grow weary, to walk and not be faint.

Love Hopes All Things

DEBBIE HERBECK

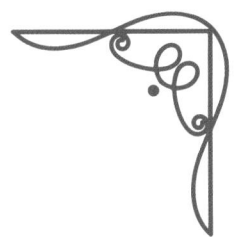

To My Younger Self,

Right now your days seem long, but trust me, the years will fly by! I'm a grandma now; it is a delightful role that allows me to enjoy the fruits of my motherhood as a helper, cheerleader, and friend to our adult children.

As I reflect on the past 37 years of motherhood, there is so much I could say as you navigate these wonderfully promising, yet challenging years. Right now, each day you are learning your vocation in the School of Love. Daily instruction in this School comes from our Lord, who is the most qualified Teacher, through his Mother, who is the best Jewish Mama, from the saints who have finished the race, and through your husband, who is striving to love you as Christ loved the Church.

I realize this letter might be difficult for you to receive, but I promise I will be gentle. I know you are battling discouragement and hope can be hard to hold.

Your prayer journals from these hands-on years of motherhood are sprinkled with spiritual insights and consolations, but also with times of discouragement. You are in those early years of your marriage and motherhood, and no matter how hard you try or how much you pray, you struggle to see eternal value in the hidden, mundane, and often thankless tasks of your daily life with little ones. In the hiddenness, you experience a nagging fear: Am I doing enough for my kids? Does what I do really matter? Could someone else do it better? The battle between your self-reliance and dependence on God rages daily, and in the midst of your mess, God comes to you with encouragement and hope.

I know you will never forget the life-changing experience at the conference in Germany. Recall it often and allow this memorable encounter to help your heart see, in a new way, the eternal value of motherhood. I believe God will also give you opportunities in the future to encourage other women as you share this story with them.

From the moment we arrived in Germany, everything seemed to go wrong. My excitement and anticipation were quickly extinguished, and amidst my fatigue and disappointment, I tearfully asked Jesus, "Why am I here? Wouldn't it be easier to just stay home?"

On the last day, resigned to defeat, an invitation unexpectedly came for a few young moms with babies to join the keynote speaker on stage. It was Mother Teresa of Calcutta! Afterward, as I bent low to greet her, she pressed a Miraculous Medal in my hand and traced the sign of the cross on my baby's forehead. As I turned to go, she pulled me closer and, looking deeply into my eyes, she said: "Never forget that although your job as a mother is difficult, it is the most important job in the whole world!"

Do you remember the certainty of that moment, of knowing exactly why you were there? Without a doubt, God used Mother Teresa to speak a word into your heart that you couldn't receive from those who loved you at home. God was answering the deeper questions of your heart as Mother Teresa dropped a seed of hope into your dry and weary soul. Back home, you

read everything you could about Mother Teresa's life and her teachings. God sent you Mother Teresa, a saint who loved faithfully even in great darkness, to teach you how to love.

This is where supernatural hope, planted in the soil of doing small things with great love, slowly begins to sprout and bear fruit. This new understanding of your vocation to love, and the small, practical ways you are learning to express this love in your family is changing your perspective on your role as a mother. As you practice smiling, loving the person right in front of you, and humbly allow yourself to be like a little pencil in the hand of God, you will truly believe that changing the world begins by loving your family.

My prayer for you is that this new way of loving will fill you with deeper hope as you discover the eternal value of your motherhood. You have a mission from God to nurture and care for not only the physical lives of your children, but to help shape their souls and their eternal destiny. What matters most isn't that you complete tasks or keep your children safe and well-fed, but that you image God's love for them in a profound and irreplaceable way. As you learn how to love through sacrificial giving in imitation of Jesus, not looking for recognition or reward, your motherhood is unfolding to you as a gift and a privilege, not as a burden or chore.

The struggle to keep this hope alive will be real as you face your own fears, deficiencies, and the fragmented pieces of your past. I see you with the eyes of compassion because I know all too

You have a mission from God to nurture and care for not only the physical lives of your children, but to help shape their souls and their eternal destiny.

well that your wounds and the persistent voice of shame make it difficult for you to believe that you can love well.

Do you remember that afternoon? Peter was traveling, and you were home all week with three children under five. You were physically exhausted and emotionally frayed. Your three-year-old son grabbed a plastic picture frame, stood in front of you, gleefully snapped it in half, and ran off to play. In that moment, something deep within you threatened to break as well. Instead of handling the situation with maturity and objectivity, you withdrew emotionally into a confusing jumble of frustration, anger, and discouragement. And then, as if waiting in the wings to confirm your fear, a dangerous but familiar lie raced through your mind: "You will never be a good mother."

But it wasn't the enemy of your soul that had the last word that day. God stepped into your brokenness and the voice of Merciful

Love clearly proclaimed to you: "You are my precious child, and by My grace and with My help, you can be a good mother and a powerful instrument of My love."

I am so proud of the ways you have begun to take down walls and let others in to share your pain. This does not disqualify you from loving well. Be patient with yourself as you seek out healing, and ask the Lord for the grace to forgive anyone in your past who failed to show you the ways of love—to forgive sooner than later. God loves the person you are right now, just as much as he loves the person you are becoming.

If you study and meditate on the Scriptures daily, over time your vocation of love will become deeply rooted in God's promises, and not in your emotions or your circumstances. As you choose gratitude instead of complaints or comparison, those seeds of hope will be nourished.

These are just a few of my favorite verses that you can memorize and claim as God's promises over your life and your family.

"I lift up my eyes up to the hills. From where does my help come from? My help comes from the Lord, who made heaven and earth" (Psalm 121:1–2).

"If God is for us, who is against us?" (Romans 8:31).

"Who shall separate us from the love of Christ? ... in all things we are more than conquerors through him who loved us" (Romans 8:35, 37).

As you welcome each day as an opportunity to love the person right in front of you, and as you faithfully say yes to the small things, the fruits of the Holy Spirit will grow and be evident in your life. The hidden nature of your vocation, and even your own weaknesses, will no longer have the power to discourage you, but rather you will experience joy as you show up each day with a heart ready to love.

Like so much of life, as soon as you settle into mothering your little ones, the landscape will begin to change (kids do grow up fast!), and the demands and challenges of motherhood will shift. There will be days when you will feel like the Israelites who stood on the edge of the Promised Land with reports of "giants in the land." Questions will arise about the future, and you will be tempted to lose heart and give in to fear. Will you have enough money for Catholic education? How will you navigate the teen years and the cultural minefields? Will your kids love Jesus and make their faith their own? Will they find a spouse who loves Jesus? In the face of all the perils ahead, do not lose sight of God's goodness and his promises.

When you feel overwhelmed by the future, read Matthew 19:25–27 and allow yourself to be encouraged by Jesus' words. The disciples are stunned, and perhaps even discouraged by how difficult and demanding it is to follow Jesus and to enter the kingdom of God. But Jesus looks at them and reminds all of us, "With men this is impossible, but with God all things are possible."

In the days ahead you will need to be reminded that without him it is impossible for you to help your children walk and grow

Claim and do not relinquish your spiritual authority as a mother.

in the way of life that leads to true and everlasting happiness. When you are tempted to try to control the outcomes for your children—academically, socially, or spiritually, remember that with God all things are possible, and you have nothing to fear.

Even now, you can begin to relinquish the illusion of "control." Claim and do not relinquish your spiritual authority as a mother. Learn how to fight—not against flesh and blood but "against the principalities, against the powers, against the world rulers of this present darkness, against the spiritual hosts of wickedness in the heavenly places" (Ephesians 6:12). Be a fierce, courageous warrior and stand in the gap for each child as they

Looking back, I now see more clearly what God was building within me throughout these years, each step vital to the next.

face temptations and are in danger of losing sight of their true identity. Pray, intercede, and teach them how to use their God-given authority to fight for themselves.

There will be those momentous "first" events, especially for your oldest child, which will signal independence—being a new driver, attending a school dance, traveling to a sports tournament, and going to college. In all these unchartered waters, all you will think about is getting that child home safe and sound. You will have a myriad of earthly goals for your children, but never forget that the greatest goal and challenge of your motherhood is to help them make it safely home to heaven. A few simple things have helped me stay the course:

- Try to remember that you can't expect your children to go one direction, if you are going in another, and no one sniffs out hypocrisy faster than our own kids.

- If you have questions, seek out the answers; if you are struggling, ask for help.
- You cannot help your children grow in their love for Jesus if you aren't making time to invest in your own spiritual growth.
- In everything you do, especially when you are in the midst of a storm, never lose sight of the one overriding goal and the ultimate destination of heaven; this is where your anchor of hope must firmly reside.

Looking back, I now see more clearly what God was building within me throughout these years, each step vital to the next. St. Paul describes this process when he writes:

"Endurance produces character, and character produces hope, and hope does not disappoint us, because God's love has been poured into our hearts through the Holy Spirit who has been given to us" (Romans 5:4–5).

I recently found a journal entry from several years ago when our last child left home. It was entitled "Things I Would Do Differently." Many years ago, that type of list would have been tinged with regret and disappointment. But reflecting backward is no longer perilous; instead, it is affirming and filled with gratitude. Without a doubt, there are many things I could have done better. But through a love that always hopes, I can now confidently proclaim that my mother's heart was strong—full of love for my children.

You won't love perfectly, but as you surrender everything to him—your weaknesses, fears, and wavering hope, he will use it all for his purpose and plan for your children. One day you will stand in my place, and you will confidently say as I do now: hope has not disappointed me!

"For now we see in a mirror dimly, but then face to face. Now I know in part; then I shall understand fully, even as I have been fully understood. So faith, hope, love abide, these three; but the greatest of these is love" (1 Corinthians 13:12–13).

Love,
YOUR OLDER SELF

- PRAYER -

*Heavenly Father, thank you
for being the sustaining hope I need.
With the deaths of Good Fridays of my life,
I will sit in hope of the resurrection that you promise.
All the fractured parts of me can often feel unhealable,
but it is through the scars you bore upon your hands
that I find hope in the transformed beauty of my wounds.
Please allow my hope in you to renew my motherhood
and open me to abounding and Christ-like love.
Allow me to meet you in these deep and intimate places
so that it will breathe life into my life,
my children's lives,
and the beating heart of my family.
I will come for you, Lord.
I will meet you there and experience
what St. Augustine said, "In my deepest wound
I saw your glory and it dazzled me."*

Amen.

Love Endures All Things

Patient endurance is
the perfection of charity.

ST. AMBROSE

"By your endurance you will gain your lives" (Luke 21:19). These eight words, which have been carefully strewn together on a small letter board, rest at the center of my kitchen for every passing eye to read. As part of our homeschooling day, the children and I recite the Bible passage of the month every morning until the truth of the words has been gently sown into the depths of their hearts. Yet, I am beginning to see that maybe these words were meant more for this mother as she moves through her daily school of love than for the tiny souls in my home.

Usually rotating the Bible passage every month, I have found myself unable to replace these little white letters with new ones. Maybe they have remained for months because I am unclear about which passage we should study next, or maybe finding the five minutes to replace them seems like a daunting feat that can only be squeezed in amidst diaper changes and reading lessons. But the truth is, I suspect they have remained because they contain a message that should not escape the heart of a mother, especially this mother.

The call to persist in love is a daily, hourly, and minute-by-minute reality when shepherding little hearts and souls. The endless noise, middle-of-the-night wakings, sibling quarrels, messes, and meals, are personal invitations by Jesus to meet him in the depths of the heart where every persevering act of love can be transformed into a sanctifying moment of holiness. The ceaseless duties of motherhood call us to be on our knees

The call to persist in love is a daily, hourly, and minute-by-minute reality when shepherding little hearts and souls.

in prayer physically or proverbially in every moment of our day. This constant need to unite our hearts with Jesus reminds us to *pray without ceasing* (see 1 Thessalonians 5:16). On our knees, or at the kitchen sink, we are continually aware of our need for Christ.

The *Catechism* reminds us that "Against our dullness and laziness, the battle of prayer is that of humble, trusting, and persevering *love*" (CCC 2742, original emphasis). Motherhood does not merely afford us the option of endurance, it demands it. God in his infinite wisdom crafted motherhood in such a way that the all too alluring appeal of laziness is no longer possible. So we persevere. We may fall, we may collapse, and we may frequently get it wrong. Covered in tears, we may even find ourselves facing the unthinkable. But in every moment, he reminds us "Talitha koum!" ... *Little girl, I say to you, arise!* (see Mark 5:41). And ... we ... persevere. Strung together, it is precisely these tiny and seemingly unnoteworthy moments of cooperation with grace, these moments of holiness, which make the saints.

So I wonder. What if what we have perceived as the exhausting burden of our daily lives, is actually one of God's greatest gifts of sanctifying grace bestowed upon the heart of a mother? And if so, then how do we respond to this gift and live out a maternal love that *arises with endurance* every day and in every moment?

Perhaps a heart that has persevered toward an enduring love can help show us the way. Bonnie, a momma mentor to me, and a woman with a heart ablaze for Jesus, has journeyed through the way of endurance. After a series of painful experiences, this woman raised without a religion or a faith found herself as a divorced mother of one falling on her knees in prayer and petition. It wasn't simply finding Jesus and the Church during

What if what we have perceived
as the exhausting burden of our daily lives,
is actually one of God's greatest gifts of
sanctifying grace bestowed upon
the heart of a mother?

some of her darkest days that guided her toward an enduring love. No, remarried with seven children, it was this Catholic convert's cooperation with his love and graces that gave her the strength to move with endurance under trial after trial, miscarriage after miscarriage, and the courage to get up when the daily challenges of motherhood knocked her down. Learning how to pick herself back up, or rather *allowing* him to scoop her off the ground, is precisely the tender place where my sweet friend Bonnie Landry whispers into the heart of her younger self. It is my prayer and hope that through her gentle words, we can be reignited with the fortitude to persevere in endurance and one day earn *"the crown of life which God has promised to those who love him"* (James 1:12, emphasis added).

Love Endures All Things

BONNIE LANDRY

Dear Younger Me,

I'm going to tell you some hard things.

You will think you can't handle these things. But you will and you do. The grace that you receive in your future is not the grace you can imagine receiving. You will not ever, ever, believe the grace he has in store for you.

There are many things, twenty-something me, that you are going to endure. Perhaps the most difficult of all will be to love yourself and to see yourself as God sees you. Perhaps the most wonderful will be learning to understand that Our Lord is with you in all things. In your littleness, your pain, your sorrow, your disappointment, your angst. He is with you and you will find your peace with him. He can carry your burden and keep you upright when your knees buckle under the pressure.

Endurance in these two things, my beautiful younger me. Loving yourself the way God loves you and trusting him with everything you experience.

You, young momma, were learning endurance; like learning to walk, you had to take baby steps first. Do not be harsh and judge yourself as one who has more life experience. This is the first hard thing I must tell you: you will lose a baby. You will be angry, but God will love you through it. Ten years later, you will have two more losses. One of these will be twins. When I tell you this now, sweet younger me, you think you will die if this happens to you. You will think that your life must be over, and you will die of a broken heart.

With that first baby, slowly (slowly because you're learning to walk) you accept the loss, that God can bring something beautiful out of this. And it is not until your next child is born that you realize, with tears in your eyes and with trust in God in your heart, that it is this particular child that is meant to walk the earth with you now. The fullness of understanding comes, all in a flash—and you rejoice and name this child Isaac, laughter, because you feel like Sarah and the great gift that was bestowed on her. You were sad and angry, but through your endurance of prayer and your love of him, sweet girl, you did not die. You grew and didn't even know it.

The losses that happened ten years later were different. Christmas morning, you pulled yourself together for your children, but you knew. After the morning festivities, they found you, weeping on your bed. You were sad, so incredibly sad. Just three months later, another loss. And though it felt like your heart was breaking, you were not angry this time. It was different, but why? Then, through your tear-filled and blurry vision, you saw it. You were growing and didn't even know it. You had learned to persevere and grow in love and trust of God.

You will have a sick child. Your heart will ache for the love of that child, and you will desire to carry all the suffering yourself.

You were growing and didn't even know it.
You had learned to persevere and
grow in love and trust of God.

You will get down on your knees and beg God for this. You, who are so afraid at this moment to suffer, will beg Our Lord for the privilege and responsibility of carrying the suffering of another. You will be allowed to carry some of that suffering and you learn, through this, to offer your suffering for others. As your children grow and take on life's challenges and burdens, you will learn to offer your suffering for them. Eventually, you will *even* do this with joy.

How? How did this happen? How did you learn to love and trust God? How did you learn to endure and persevere in love? Each day, you practiced. Each day you loved to the best of your ability on that given day. You failed regularly, but every morning you woke with the intention of loving your best. You practiced. Little by little, you gained strength. You gained wisdom. You gained ability. You gained acceptance that you were a child of God, a beautiful and precious child of God. Because you practiced. Because you created good habits. And eventually, it became more natural to love yourself, love others, love God.

So I'm going to tell you this. Just practice, every day. In little ways, in little things. Practice tenderness. When you yell at the kids, remember to be gentle with yourself. When you are harsh or irritable, be tender with yourself. Remind yourself that you are small and weak and made in God's image. He will help you be more like himself. But it will take your whole life. So just remember for today. Endurance in love means willing to commit yourself to practicing in little ways every day. Every day for the rest of your life.

Practice not being angry. Just practice sitting with whatever is happening that's making you angry and see how that is. Accept little annoying things. First, start with just not reacting; eventually, you may even accept annoying things with grace … and then joy. God is in all things.

Practice loving others. Assume the best of them and treat them with the dignity that you would hope others would see in you when you are grumpy or sad or uncharitable or unreasonable. Quiet your heart and really listen to what they

are saying without trying to develop your response while they are saying it. Remember why you fell in love with your husband. Remember your children as babies when you brought them into the world. Practice remembering the very best moments in your relationships.

Practice kindness. Such little ways of speaking, touching, or understanding do not take any time out of our day. Say "I love you" often. Say "thank you" often. Practice thanking your family for just doing the ordinary things they do. Mother Teresa says, "Let no one ever come to you without leaving better and happier. Be the living expression of God's kindness: kindness in your face, kindness in your eyes, kindness in your smile."

Practice courage. It takes a lot of courage to be a Christian. To tell the truth, to share the Gospel. To be open to children. But these are big things, and we always need to start with small things. Sometimes just getting up in the morning takes all the courage we can muster. When you feel that little angst creeping up inside you because a hard thing is ahead of you … remember to pray, "Satan, get thee behind me." Practice remembering that Our Lord is always with you. Practice praying when you need it the most, in moments of fear and angst. St. Philip Neri said, "Paradise was not made for cowards." Oh, be brave, younger me.

Practice patience. Oh, patience, elusive patience, where are you when we need you most? When the juice spills. When

It takes a lot of courage to be a Christian.
To tell the truth, to share the Gospel.
To be open to children. But these are
big things, and we always need
to start with small things.

the dog escapes the yard. When the children are bickering. When the toddler is whining. When dinner burns. Breathe. Breathe deeply. It calms you and helps you think more clearly. Breathing allows that slim moment to let the Holy Spirit into your response. Practice pausing before reacting. Practice the devotion of the Three Hail Marys. When you feel like you are going to explode, react, or pounce, breathe and pray. Then respond. Breathing and praying will still you, steady you, and make you ready to respond instead of exploding, reacting, or pouncing.

Practice loving yourself. A little critical voice sometimes creeps into your thoughts. You are not fit enough. You are not smart enough. You are not worthy of love. You are a phony. Please, sweet young me, so full of enthusiasm for your children and life, look at yourself. Look at yourself with the eyes of God. Look, just look at the exquisite creation he made! Practice looking at yourself the way you look at your new baby. Appreciate the beauty and wonder with which he has created you. To let those thoughts creep into your mind is to not allow God to be God! Let him be the master, creative genius, life-giving, perfect God that he is by practicing seeing yourself as he sees you. As he made you.

Practice every day. Practice some small thing every day so that that habit—the virtue—of perseverance becomes a part of your daily walk. Endurance is such a fundamental and overlooked aspect of growth in holiness. Our Lord just wants to draw us to him, one step forward at a time. Every time we practice, we have made one more movement closer to him. And all the saints and angels in heaven rejoice to see us drawing into our life in Our Lord.

And here's what I've observed, younger me, as I've watched you grow. You have grown closer to God and your eternal life, and as a beautiful consequence, you have also grown in your earthly life and relationships. You are happier. You are more content. You are more patient. You are more willing to accept what is. One step at a time, you are inching your way toward perfect happiness and perfect love. Heaven awaits you, my love, my younger me.

You will suffer many things, and you will have so much joy, more joy than your poor heart can hold. You will be so aware of the blessed life you have lived and the richness of this world. You will develop gratitude because you persevered in love and prayer. And one day, when your biggest trial of life to this point comes, you will know that God has become such a part of your daily walk that you are willing to accept even this. And *even* find an enduring joy in it.

Love,

FUTURE YOU

- PRAYER -

*Heavenly Father, thank you
for revealing my need for you.
When the days are thick with exhaustion and tears,
please give me the grace to remember that my human eyes
can only see the cross of the current moment,
while you see the glory of my entire life.
You, all-knowing, have always known
the beauty that is born from my endurance.
When I feel too small to handle all that I face,
please, Jesus, give me the wisdom to know
that I am indeed too small and the understanding
to see that this is where true freedom lies.
For alone I can do nothing, but instead
"I can do all things in him who strengthens me"
(Philippians 4:13). Most importantly, give me the strength
and courage to pursue a life that
perseveres with love for you!*

Amen.

Love Never Fails

Love is the most beautiful sentiment that the Lord has put into the soul of men and women.

ST. GIANNA MOLLA

In today's world of information overload, we mommas are often inundated with thousands of competing messages that advise us on how to best care for the little souls in our homes. We become overwhelmed with the numerous ways to educate, cook, console, play, discipline, encourage, adventure, and accompany our children through this short life on this side of heaven's veil. In fact, there are almost as many variations to motherhood as there were Jewish laws while the Son of Man walked this earth.

We mommas, like the Jews in their time, simply want to *get it right*. It must have been overwhelming for the people of Israel to try to live a life for God while abiding by the hundreds of laws contained within the Torah. So, I find myself full of compassion when the nameless scribe asks Jesus, "Which commandment is the first of all?" (Mark 12:28). What should he spend his time on, which commandment should he be most disciplined about, and which law should he take back to his home with him and honor with the greatest reverence? I fall on my knees and ask the Lord the same question. *Which way of motherhood is best? Of all the ways to shepherd my children, tell me, which is the first of all?*

Jesus answers both the scribe and this seeking mom's heart, when he says, "The first is...*you shall love the Lord your God with all your heart, and with all your soul, and with all your mind, and with all your strength.' The second is this, 'You shall love your neighbor as yourself.'* There is no other commandment greater than these" (Mark 12:29–31).

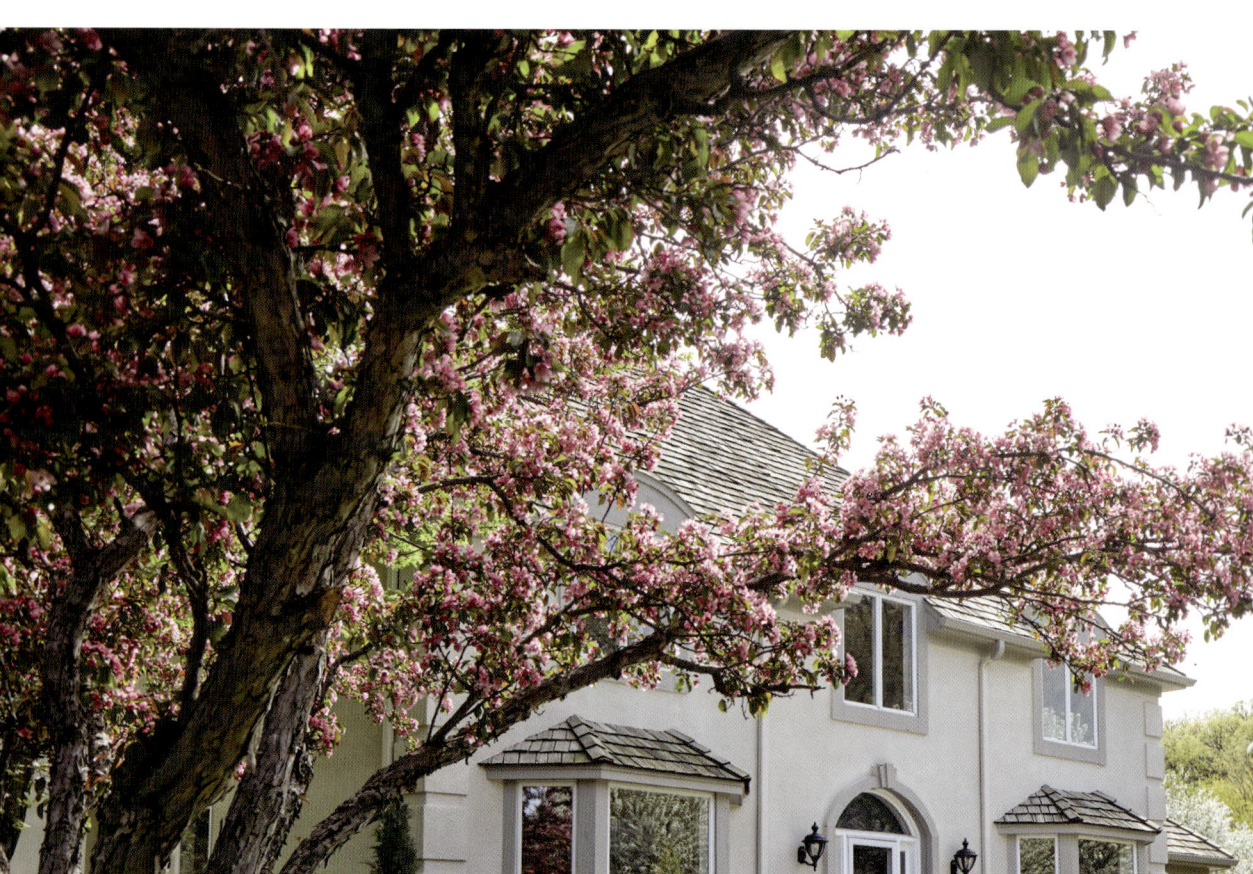

With these few words, Jesus in his magnificence strips off over 600 heavy layers of details and leaves the scribe naked and exposed to the greatest truth of God's heart—love, period. First, love God, and second, love your neighbor; your neighbor in the crib, your neighbor at the kitchen table, your neighbor who climbs in and out of your lap, and your neighbor out in the back rolling around in the sand and dirt.

But in a sea of worry, our fear frequently distracts our hearts from this greater mission. We, like Martha, can become overwhelmed with many things, such as how to best feed (sugar-free, gluten-free, vegan, or high protein), to best educate (public school, private school, or homeschool), or to best socialize (sports, sleepovers, or after-school activities) these little neighbors. Yet, Jesus makes it clear. Motherhood is not just a series of choices to be made to mold the perfect product. Perhaps we were never called to simply *get it right*. Instead, as God ordained, it is a vocation of leading little hearts in love, through love, and toward love. It is a journey of nurturing and training the hearts and minds of little souls so that one day they will reside in eternal paradise *with Love* himself.

But with an ocean of resources, thousands of books on motherhood, and all of the how-tos we are drowning in, how can we trust that our motherhood could be as simple as the two great commandments? Because Love himself said so. Period. Love, who washed our feet, restored sight to the blind, and raised men from the dead, tells us that love is the answer. Lucky for us sweet mommas, Jesus not only whispers the key to unlocking our maternal splendor—love—but he also assures our wary hearts that this way will never fail.

Machines fail, initiatives fail, trails end, and sadly all too often, friendships end, but the love that abounds from the birthplace of goodness itself can never fail and will never end. It is sourced from Love himself who is never ending nor changing (see Malachi 2:17). "I have loved you with an *everlasting love*; therefore I have continued my faithfulness to you" (Jeremiah 31:3, emphasis added).

As I near the end of this exploration of love in motherhood, I'm in awe with a full heart about the pure *simplicity* of what Christ has called us to. **LOVE**. When our eyes stay fixed on loving our Lord, commandment one, how can we not overflow with his abounding love for those around us, commandment two? It is his Love alive in us that scratches their backs and tussles their hair, who feeds those little mouths, and whose body stretches and aches with maternal capacity. It is Love who carries, nurses, chauffeurs, teaches, and guides. It is Love who looks them in the eyes and asks for forgiveness.

Love cannot be defeated. You can scourge his body, strip him naked, nail him to a cross, and suffocate him to death, but Love will never end nor fail. No, sweet momma, Love wins, for it came and conquered the world with two arms stretched out wide.

So how can we keep our hearts steadfast on a mission of a never-failing love? How can we remember to soak in the grandeur of the love that God has infused into our maternal hearts? Perhaps a mother who was stripped of secondary matters, just as the scribe was, as she spent years dedicated to the primary job of love, can breathe life into the young mom's heart. A beautiful momma of two, the lovely Mary Lenaburg has walked through the way of love. She has learned the painful yet glorious lesson that love never fails, even at the point of death. It is my prayer that her words will encourage you to step into the love that God has called you to. In a world that distracts our minds and consumes our hearts with many things, I pray Mary's letter will remind you of the "better way" and the great truth that "faith, hope, love abide, these three; but the greatest of these is love" (1 Corinthians 13:13).

Love Never Fails

MARY LENABURG

Hey Sis,

Grab a cup of coffee or tea if you like and come and sit with me a minute. I want to share something with you, something that's been etched in my heart and soul through this journey of motherhood.

Sis, I am so proud of you. Seriously, you're in the midst of an incredible adventure, fulfilling those childhood dreams, brimming with hope, and I have no doubt a touch of trepidation. But trust me when I say that you are more than ready for what lies ahead. I know your knees go weak at the thought of caring for and loving children that are so completely different from one another as Jonathan and Courtney are, that need you in ways you never thought possible. Take a breath, sis. Now take another.

Take a moment and truly soak it in. This beautiful adventure, this dream you've held close since you were holding baby dolls, swept you off your feet and has filled your heart with a love so profound you find yourself short of breath at times. It's OK. God's got you. He's holding you close; lean in and listen to his heartbeat. That's the secret. St Paul writes, "Love never fails" (1 Corinthians 13:8 NAB). Since God is love, and he cannot fail, then it must be true, right?

Oh yes, friend. It's one thing I know for sure. Love never fails.

Imagine this, you're walking on a picturesque path through a lush forest, dappled with sunlight and resounding with the sweet symphony of birdsong. Each step you take will lead you deeper into the heart of motherhood, where the air is thick with wonder, laughter, and the scent of baby lotion. It's a path where you'll discover hidden springs of resilience within yourself, where you'll bloom like a wildflower in the meadow of love.

I know it sounds magical, and at times it is, until it isn't.

There will be moments when you feel like you're scaling a mountain, each step more challenging than the last. There will be times when you question if you have what it takes to navigate the twists and turns ahead. But hold onto this truth like a lifeline—love never fails. You are not alone. Love will be your steadfast companion, your guiding light, and your source of unwavering strength.

I want you to know that you are more than equipped for the journey ahead. You possess a reservoir of love within you that knows no bounds. It's a love that will carry you through sleepless nights, diaper disasters, and teenage tantrums. It's a love that will heal scraped knees, mend broken hearts, and create a safe haven within your home.

A safe haven is all you've ever desired.

But before we dive deeper into the beautiful intricacies of motherhood, let's talk about those meticulous plans you've crafted—you know, the ones where every expectation is neatly tied with a bow. You've always been the planner extraordinaire, haven't you? But let me drop a little knowledge bomb on you, straight from the archives of Grandma Stuecken's trunk of

Love will be your steadfast companion, your guiding light, and your source of unwavering strength.

wisdom: "Hold loosely to your plans and allow the Holy Spirit to work." Life has a wicked sense of humor, and motherhood? You can plan all you want, but life will toss curveballs your way. Some of the most magical moments happen when you least expect them. Trust me on this one; your heart's in for a wild ride.

Now, let's chat fear and faith—your two old frenemies. Fear likes to play the control freak, while faith is all about freedom. Fear hates Faith because Fear is control and Faith is freedom. Fear doesn't come from God; it's like a pesky mosquito at a summer barbecue, buzzing in your ear, trying to steal your peace. You'll have moments of doubt, especially as you step into the unknown territory as a mother. But here's the deal—have faith in God, in yourself, and in the beautiful journey that's unfolding. When you kick fear to the curb and let faith lead the way, you'll find a newfound freedom that'll light up your path. "With God, all things are possible."

Motherhood is often a whirlwind, a cyclone of chaos and cuddles. There will be days when you'll question your sanity and wonder if you're doing it all right. During those moments, remember Mom's golden rule: "Love the person right in front of you and just do the next right thing." Your to-do list may resemble a never-ending novel, but don't let it become your obsession. Pour your love into the one who needs it most at that moment, whether it's your newborn's midnight feeding, a toddler's epic meltdown, or a teenager in search of advice. Focus on the next right thing, and you'll navigate even the wildest of days. That's the essence of love, choosing to do good for the one before you.

Savor the moments, sis. "Be where your feet are planted," as they say. Those quiet moments when you hold your little one close or share a bedtime story. It will be etched in your memory forever. Time will slip through your fingers like sand, and those small moments will be your most precious treasures. So, be fully present, dear sister, and soak in the beauty of the now. It's these moments that'll carry you through the stormier days.

Let's get practical for a moment. You know those moments of everyday life that still make your cringe, those mundane tasks you hate—the endless loads of laundry, the never-ending cycle of dishes, and the bathroom floors that seem to attract messes like magnets—those are an opportunity to offer something beautiful to the world. You may wonder, "What's so special about scrubbing floors or folding laundry?" Well, sis, God wastes nothing. Every diaper changed, every meal prepared, every bedtime story read, and every scraped knee kissed can be offered up as an act of love. It's in these seemingly ordinary moments that you'll find the extraordinary. So, when you're knee-deep in the chaos of everyday life, remember that every opportunity is a chance to love, to serve, and to make a difference in the lives of your precious little ones. Love never fails, and God uses even the smallest acts of love to weave a tapestry of beauty and grace, and boy does it change your heart.

It's time to dig a little deeper into the next layer of this heart-to-heart, a chapter that's a cornerstone of who you are. Let's talk about Courtney, our girl, our warrior, our light. For twenty-two years, she will grace your life, redefining the very essence of strength and love.

Courtney isn't just a daughter; she is a force that will defy every medical textbook, every whispered doubt. She is fiercely herself

> **Love never fails, and God uses even the smallest acts of love to weave a tapestry of beauty and grace, and boy does it change your heart.**

in a world that didn't know how to contain such purity of spirit. Yes, sis, she will be medically fragile and severely disabled, but that's just medical jargon. To you, to us, she is Courtney, the girl who communicates worlds of love without saying a word, whose laughter will be a symphony that echoes through the walls of your home, turning each day into a melody of joy.

Being Courtney's mom, your greatest challenge? Absolutely. But, oh, the gift of it, the sheer, unadulterated gift. Every smile, every moment of connection is a treasure chest of joy, isn't it? It will be hard, hands down, the hardest thing you will ever do. But each time she smiles, it will be like the dawn breaking after the darkest night, reminding you that joy comes in the morning.

Courtney's life is a masterclass in love, teaching you that the heart has no limits. Each day with her will be a lesson in patience, in resilience, and in finding the joy in the smallest things—the way the sun lights up her face, or how she grips your hand with a strength that belied her fragility.

Remember this, as you wipe away the tears and power through the sleep-deprived nights: you were chosen for each other, by a God who knows your fortitude, who sees the vast expanse of your heart. You and Courtney, together, are a testament to the unyielding power of a mother's love.

And let's be real, the sass and spirit that got you through the door-slamming teenage years? That's the same fire you carry now, the same fire that lights up Courtney's world. The love you pour into her, into every therapy session, every doctor's visit, it's revolutionary. It's the stuff of miracles.

So, when the weight of 'what ifs' tries to steal your breath, stand firm in the knowledge that you are exactly where you need to be. Loving Courtney and her big brother Jonathan is your superpower, your calling, your breathtaking journey back to the heart of what matters most. Through every challenge, every heartache, and every moment of pure, unfiltered happiness, love is your compass.

And remember, sis, when the days are long and the years feel like they're slipping through your fingers, when you're standing by the bedside of a world that doesn't understand the depth of your journey—you're not just surviving; you're teaching the world about love. Courtney's legacy is written in the hearts she will touch, in the lives she will change, and in the unbreakable bond you share.

Speaking of unbreakable bond, let's not forget your partner in crime—your husband, the grouchy one. In the grand spectacle of motherhood, he's your leading man, your confidant, and the love of your life. Don't forget to love him well amidst the chaos. Lean on each other, laugh together, and hold hands through the ups and downs. In this grand adventure, it's you two against the world. Choose love, choose each other, and remember, love never fails.

Before I forget, the infamous comparison game—it's a trap you fall into along the way. Remember the hard lesson you learned in the sixth grade. Keep your eyes on your own paper. Your family and your marriage have a unique story unlike any other. Embrace that journey, those triumphs, as well as your struggles. Comparing yourself to others only robs you of the joy of your own adventure. Stay true to your path, love your beautiful babies, and cherish the love and connection within your family. It's life-giving and changes your heart in a radical way.

Finally, when your heart is shattered and death comes to your doorstep, and trials and tribulations are pounding on your door—let the tears come, sis. Feel all the feels. Don't fight them or lock them away. Remember what I said. Love never fails. God

will give you the wisdom, strength, and grace to walk through them. You are never alone. I know that you will struggle with that, and the crushing of your heart will feel unsurvivable, and the grief will overwhelm you on the daily, but oh my girl, God is faithful and true.

I need you to look at me and nod your head, sis. Did you hear me?

God is faithful and true, and you are strong and brave, and you need to remember that love never fails because love is the whole

> **God's love is unwavering, and his grace will be your guiding light.**

reason you're here. You can love because God loved you first. He showed you the way, so just keep putting one foot in front of the other and keep loving.

God makes beautiful things from the ashes, so stand in faith and don't quit. Those trials may feel like heavy burdens; lean on your faith and your friends, seek solace in prayer, and trust that you possess the inner strength to conquer any obstacle. God's love is unwavering, and his grace will be your guiding light. Love will not fail you, sis.

So, my dear sister, as you continue this remarkable journey as Mother, hold onto these truths: let your plans be flexible, let faith triumph over fear, love wholeheartedly, be present in the moment, trust in God's wisdom and grace, and stay true to your unique path.

Let's not just stroll through motherhood, sis; let's dance through it with hearts wide open. Let's revel in the late-night cuddles, the first steps, and the whispered bedtime stories. Embrace the chaos of spilled cereal, muddy footprints, and finger-painted masterpieces on multi-colored construction paper. Let's celebrate the awkward laughter and the wheelchair races. Because amid it all, love will weave a tapestry of memories that will adorn the walls of your heart. Keep on loving, keep on fighting, and above all, keep on shining, just like our girl did. You're destined for greatness, dear sister, and remember, in the whirlwind of motherhood, in the eye of the storm, there is always, always love.

Love is the fiercest weapon we have. It never fails. It is the beginning and the end, the alpha and the omega of our journey. Dance through this wild, wonderful life with Courtney's memory as your rhythm, and let love lead the way. It's a dance that never ends, for love—true, boundless, fearless love—it never fails.

With Love,
OLDER YOU

- PRAYER -

*Lord, thank you
for showering me with
a never-ending kind of love.
Please give me the grace to remember
that "if I speak in the tongues of men and of angels,
but have not love, I am a noisy gong or a clanging cymbal.
And if I have prophetic powers, and understand all mysteries
and all knowledge, and if I have all faith,
so as to remove mountains, but have not love, I am nothing.
If I give away all I have, and if I deliver up my body
to be burned, but have not love, I gain nothing"
(1 Corinthians 13:1–3). Please help orient my heart
and soul toward the only thing that
never ends nor ever fails—Love;
Love of God and of neighbor.
And let my entire life be an outpouring of these two
great commandments, especially in my own home.*

Amen.

One More Note ...

Shortly after the idea of *She Loved* blossomed in my heart, I began gradually encountering the beautiful women that would one day write in it. Over time, I became overwhelmed with a sense of gratitude for the vulnerability and tenderness of their maternal hearts. Then the letters began to come in. My voice would choke and my eyes would swell with tears as I'd read aloud to my husband an outpouring from a momma's heart. "If God never desires to publish this book," I'd say, "this mom heart is collecting a treasure trove of maternal beauty, goodness, and wisdom. In a completely new way, I feel seen and known."

In writing this book and reading these letters, my eyes have been opened, my heart has been stretched, and my soul has been renewed with maternal hope. More than ever, I am confident that God is on a mission, with the intercession of Momma Mary, to restore, revive, and reclaim the vocation of motherhood. Right here. Right now. At this time. And he is reclaiming it through *you*—with *your* hands that wash that shirt, wipe that tear, push that stroller, scrub that dish, twirl that dancing child, and scoop up that little one. He is on the move at your kitchen sink, in your nursery, in your car, and deep into the dark of night when no one else sees or hears the love of your motherhood. He is ON MISSION, with *you*. As you journey on this mission with the Lord, I invite you to pause and pray for his blessings over your motherhood, right here, right now, and along the road of your maternity. Specifically, I have included a powerful "Litany for Motherhood" at the end of this book as a beautiful tool and heart cry to the heavens for your mother heart.

It is my deep prayer, a prayer that was born from my own maternal heart cry, that the words in this book find their way into the blood within your veins, the beat within your heart, and the magnificence within your soul. I hope that it not only blesses you here and now, but that it serves as a timeless treasure of maternal solidarity and encouragement that your aging hands and eyes will come back to over the days and years. I pray that when your heart grows weary, which it will, the words strewn through these pages will be a way for the moms who wrote them to come alongside you, wipe your tears, and remind you of *your* belovedness, *your* goodness, and the profound calling of *your* motherhood for *your* children. Let these words encourage you on the way, the only way, the *way of love*.

And then one day ... after all of the messes and beauty, the sorrows and joys, the imperfections and triumphs of your motherhood, it will be said, "Job well done" ..."for **she loved much**" (Luke 7:47, emphasis added).

- LITANY FOR MOTHERHOOD -

*For growth in the virtues of patience and gentleness,
Mary, Mother of God, guide me*

*For the peace of Christ to control my heart,
Mary, Mother of God, guide me*

*To love without counting the cost,
Mary, Mother of God, guide me*

To practice self-control in healthy ways instead of anger or bitterness, Mary, Mother of God, guide me

*To find joy in both the big and little moments,
Mary, Mother of God, guide me*

*To live holy in the present moment,
Mary, Mother of God, guide me*

*From the desire of perfectionism in myself and my children,
Deliver me Jesus*

*From comparison of my journey as a mother,
Deliver me Jesus*

*From the lie that I am not worthy,
Deliver me Jesus*

*From discouragement in my vocation,
Deliver me Jesus*

From anxiety and giving into insecurities,
Deliver me Jesus

From wanting control,
Deliver me Jesus

That you are with me in my vocation as a mother,
Jesus, I trust in you

That I am content with what you provide my family,
Jesus, I trust in you

That I am able to put my children's needs above my own,
Jesus, I trust in you

That each day I find a grateful heart,
Jesus, I trust in you

That I give cheerfully to my children,
Jesus, I trust in you

That I can surrender my vocation over to you,
Jesus, I trust in you

— MARIE LOESEL, *ABUNDANCE OF GRACE PRINTS* —

Acknowledgments

To my Heavenly Father, who has loved me enough to call me worthy of loving the people in my home. To my beloved hubby, Paul, who has given me the courage to love our children well. Thank you for being my encourager, my best friend, and the captain of joy in our home. Not only have you let me sneak out to far too many coffee shops to write, but more importantly you have lavished me with a restoring kind of love. To the other loves of my life, my children, who inspired this book, my motherhood to you is the deepest joy of my heart. To Mom, Mom B., and my sisters, you have blessed me with your love, care, and vulnerable hearts. To my sweet nieces for your tender and always timely encouragement. To my cheerleaders, Sara, Julia, Beth, Carrie, Johnna, Janine, Liv, and my beloved COWs—McKenzie, Bridget, and Angela—without your capacity to love, be loved, and encourage, this book would have never been possible. To my beloved Higganum crew, for showing me what it means to belong to a family. For the women who have poured out their hearts throughout the pages of this book. The gift of your words has already penetrated the depths of my maternal heart and reignited me with a mission of love and motherhood. I am confident that your words will bless every mother who turns the pages of this book. Finally, to Lori Miller, Jessica Walters, Meredith Wilson, Katelyn Servey, Ashley Dias, and the entire team at Ascension, thank you for the gift of your hearts and the passion that you carry for the soul of the woman. You have been nothing but a blessing for this project, this mission, and this girl's heart. Thank you for trusting me with this grand mission and for taking a leap of faith on this unworthy first-time author.

NOTES

1. József Mindszenty, *The Mother* (Post Falls, ID: Lepanto Press, 2008), 65–66.
2. See Heather McCargo, "Growing Ramps from Seed," Maine Organic Farmers and Gardeners, updated March 8, 2021, mofga.org.
3. See Calvin Norman and Cathryn Pugh, "Ramps (*Allium tricoccum*)," Penn State Extension, updated March 20, 2023, extension.psu.edu.
4. Mother Teresa, *Heart of Joy: The Transforming Power of Self-Giving* (Edmond, OK: Servant, 1987), 120.
5. *Cambridge Dictionary*, "kindness," accessed August 8, 2024, dictionary.cambridge.org.
6. Cyprian of Carthage, "Jealousy and Envy," *Treaty 10*, chapter 1, ewtn.com, emphasis added.
7. Rick Warren, *The Purpose Driven Life* (Grand Rapids, MI: Zondervan, 2012), 262.
8. John Paul II, "Letter to Women" (June 29, 1995), vatican.va.
9. See "Science of Memory," John Hopkins Medicine, accessed August 8, 2024, hopkinsmedicine.org.
10. See Michelle Pereira, "Why Do Bad Memories Last Longer?" *Science ABC* (October 2023), scienceabc.com.
11. Good News Translation of the Bible, available from Pauline.org.
12. John Paul II, Apostolic Voyage to Toronto: Mass for the Celebration of the 17th World Youth Day in Downsview Park, Toronto: Homily (July 28, 2002), 5, vatican.va, original emphasis.
13. See Oliver J. Bosch, "Maternal Aggression in Rodents: Brain Oxytocin and Vasopressin Mediate Pup Defence," *Philosophical Transactions of the Royal Society B: Biological Sciences* 368, no. 1631 (December 5, 2013).
14. Thérèse of Lisieux, "Letter 197 to Sister Marie of the Sacred Heart (September 17, 1896)" in *Letters II: 1890–1897* (Washington, DC: ICS, 1988), 1000.
15. Benedict XVI, *Spe salvi* (November 30, 2007), 1, vatican.va, emphasis added.

BIBLIOGRAPHY

Ayre, Melinda. (2017) *The Secret Behind Your Mama Bear Instinct.* Honey Nine. honey.nine.com.au.

Callaway, Linda. (Sept. 2023). *The Origin of the Word "Kind": Etymology and History.* Symbol Genie. symbolgenie.com.

Cambridge Dictionary. (2024) *Kindness - English Meaning.*

Lincoln, Abraham. *Quotes About Kindness.* Compassion. compassion.com.

Long, Li. Minghui, Yu. Wenjing, Yao. Yulong, Ding. Shuyan, Lin. (Dec. 2023) *Research Advance in Growth and Development of Bamboo Organs.* Science Direct. sciencedirect.com.

Norman, Calvin and Pugh, Cathryn. (March 2023). *Ramps (Allium tricoccum).* Penn State Extension. extension.psu.edu.

McCargo, Heather. (2016). *Growing Ramps from Seed.* Maine Organic Farmers and Gardeners. mofga.org.

Pereira, Michelle (Oct. 2023) *Why Do Bad Memories Last Longer?* Science ABC. scienceabc.com.

Rodriguez, Roberto. (Aug. 2023). *Cornerman: Ringside Assistance in Boxing Sports.* Bamsports. bamsports.org.

Snow, Avital. (Oct. 2023). *Here am I! - The Hebrew Meaning of Hineni.* FIRM Israel. firmisrael.org.

Vatican City: Libreria Editrice Vaticana, 1997. Print. *Catechism of the Catholic Church: Revised in Accordance with the Official Latin Text Promulgated by Pope John Paul II.*

More About Us

SUZANNE BILODEAU

Suzanne Bilodeau is head over heels in love with Jesus. Wife to her high school sweetheart Paul, Suzanne is a homeschooling momma of six beautiful children. A former success-seeking actuary and a recovering perfectionist and overachiever, she encountered Christ in a new and restoring way in motherhood. Host of the popular podcast *Latte & Laundry*, Suzanne explores what it means to sit at the feet of Christ like Mary, while moving in this world with the gusto and strength of Martha. She is convicted that God is on mission to restore and revive the magnificent vocation of motherhood, and she delights in letting him use her in any tiny way he sees fit. If you can't find her in the kitchen or laundry room of her CT home, she is probably on a run, in the garden, or planning her next adventure with the kids.

ALICIA HERNON

Alicia Hernon, along with her husband Michael, are co-founders of the Messy Family Project, a ministry that is dedicated to empowering moms and dads to embrace their sacred calling. Mother of ten children and "Nonni" to eight grandchildren, Alicia, with Mike, has traveled around the world to encourage families and spark conversations between spouses on how to be the best parents for their children. Alicia and Mike offer down-to-earth, practical insights into family life through their podcast, free marriage and parenting resources, and parenting courses.

HEIDI BRATTON

Heidi Bratton is an accomplished Catholic photographer, author, and educator who loves to tell stories and evangelize through her photography. With a heart for strengthening the domestic church, Heidi has published numerous collections of photo-illustrated books for both kids and moms. As a mother of six children and with 35 years of navigating family life under her belt, Heidi has a deep desire to help other moms sail through the sometimes calm and sometimes choppy waters of motherhood ... while keeping their family boats afloat! Heidi spent over two decades in Catholic education, homeschooling her own children and working as an educational consultant at a Catholic grammar school. These days, she lives in Michigan with her husband, John, and is enjoying her new role as a Nana.

HEATHER VOCCOLA

Heather Voccola serves as Executive Director of Mary and Elizabeth, an apostolate dedicated to the interior renewal of women. She has a master's in theology and a certification in direction through Heart of Christ Spiritual Direction. She currently teaches priests, religious, seminarians, and laity through Holy Apostles College and Seminary, Avila Institute, and Stella Maris Network. Though currently living a vow of chastity to our Lord within an intentional community of female missionaries, she has two adult daughters from a prior marriage and one son-in-law; she will forever be grateful for the vocation of marriage and motherhood.

DOROTHY PILARSKI

Dorothy is on a mission to revive the vocation of motherhood, primarily by helping parishes start moms groups. After hosting her own Catholic Moms Group for over 25 years, her ministry Catholic Moms Group has helped moms groups start in Canada, the USA, and Wales. Dorothy is the host of a virtual meetup for moms called Midday Moms. She was a columnist for the *Catholic Register* and a TV host with Salt + Light TV. In her stint on Radio Maria, you might have heard her talk about her book *Motherhood Matters*. Right now she's just finished hosting the 15th annual Dynamic Women of Faith conference and is currently working on a project called *Your Life Is Going to Change*.

EMILY JAMINET

Emily Jaminet is on a mission to help Catholics be impacted by the love of Christ in their hearts and homes. She is a Catholic author, and her most recent book is *Holy Habits from the Sacred Heart*. She enjoys being a Catholic speaker, radio personality, podcaster, wife, and mother to seven children. She thanks God for the impactful Catholic pilgrimages she has gone on over the years, including the Holy Land, Rome, France, and other Marian shrines. She is now the executive director of Welcome His Heart, a ministry that helps Catholics encounter the love of Christ through the devotion to the Sacred Heart.

LISA BRENNINKMEYER

Lisa Brenninkmeyer is the founder and CEO of Walking with Purpose, a Catholic ministry providing Bible studies and authentic community for women around the country. Lisa has written Bible studies for adult women, a young adult series, a mentoring program for high school girls, a curriculum for middle school girls, and three devotionals. Lisa holds a BA in psychology from St. Olaf College and is pursuing her master's in theology from Franciscan University of Steubenville. She and her husband Leo have seven children and live in St. Augustine, Florida.

ELIZABETH FOSS

Elizabeth is a founder of Take Up Ministries and a certified Catholic life coach. She is a morning person who relishes her time alone with the Word as much as she loves deep kitchen conversations over big mugs of tea. A wife, a mother of nine, and a grandmother, she is very happy planting flowers or tinkering with a turn of phrase. Elizabeth would rather be outdoors than inside, and she especially loves venturing out in her historic Connecticut village for long walks that sometimes break into a run.

CHRISTINE DUDLEY

Upending her plan to not marry until she was forty, Christine converted to Catholicism when she was twenty-one, married at twenty-two, and became a mother at twenty-four. While having her four youngest children, she completed a law degree only to discover she preferred full-time parenting. She is the homeschooling mother of six daughters and of one son who died at age seven after a three-year experience of brain cancer. With her youngest daughter approaching adulthood, she meaningfully fills her time doing pro bono work for non-profits, pursuing work as a domestic couples mediator, and caring for her aging parents.

BETH SRI

After serving as one of the first FOCUS missionaries, Beth has mentored moms and young adults for 20+ years. She helps lead retreats for Life-Giving Wounds, a ministry for adult children of divorce, and regularly presents on prayer, healing, and motherhood. A mother of eight children, Beth has a passion for Jane Austen, distance running, and cheering for her kids at their soccer games. She and her husband Edward are authors of two books together: *Pocket Guide to Prayer* and *The Good, the Messy & the Beautiful: The Joys and Struggles of Real Married Life.*

CARRIE DAUNT

Carrie Daunt has a love for family life and a deep desire for restoration for all families. In addition to her vocation as a wife and mother, Carrie is a speaker for the John Paul II Healing Center. She is also the author of three books on identity and healing: *Undone: Freeing your Feminine Heart from the Knots of Fear and Shame, Man Your Post: Learning to Lead like St. Joseph* (co-authored with her husband, Duane), and most recently released, a children's book entitled *Beloved Daughter*. Carrie resides in Florida with her supersized family.

LAURA PHELPS

Laura Phelps is an author, speaker, and visionary leader passionate about getting women excited about their Catholic faith. After a powerful conversion in her forties, Laura has been on a mission to share the good things the Lord has done. She is a Content Creator Manager at Walking With Purpose, an Apostolate that aims to lead women to a personal encounter with Jesus through Scripture. You can listen to Laura as the co-host of *Hope For Right Now*, a Walking With Purpose Podcast. She resides in CT with her husband, four children, and way too many pets.

CHRISTINE HANUS

A lover of Jesus Christ, a wife, and a mother, Christine is the author of *Everyday Heroism: 28 Daily Reflections on the Little Way of Motherhood*. She is a graduate of Franciscan University, a writing instructor, and a long-time catechist. Christine and her husband, who have a passion for education, are currently working in a Catholic school in western Colorado. Incredibly, over the past few years, their five children have all married, and Christine and her husband have been blessed with a passel of small grandchildren.

DEBBIE HERBECK

Debbie is passionate about helping young women encounter the personal love of Jesus and empowering them to be Christ's love in the world. Raised a Jew, Debbie met Jesus in college and her whole world changed. Years later, an unexpected meeting with Mother Teresa transformed her vocation as a mother. For more than 40 years, Debbie has worked in youth and women's ministry. She is the Founder and Executive Director of Pine Hills Girls' Camp and Be Love Revolution, ministries that help young women encounter Christ. Debbie is the author of five books, including a marriage book with her husband Peter. The Herbecks live in Ann Arbor, Michigan, and have four children and twelve grandchildren.

BONNIE LANDRY

Bonnie Landry's mission is joy. Through her speaking, writing, and podcasting, she shares how we can live the challenges of family life more joyfully. Fostering dignity in relationships and giving parents tools for cozy homeschooling are the focus of her ministry. She became Catholic as an adult when she realized the immense gift of her first child; she began looking for the one who gives life and found him in the Catholic Church. Her ministry focus is through her podcast, *Make Joy Normal*, and speaking at conferences and retreats. She loves gardening and travel. As she and her husband Albert have recently retired, Bonnie spends most of her time with Albert, their grown children, and their grandchildren usually in their yard and garden on Vancouver Island.

MARY LENABURG

Mary Lenaburg is a devoted wife of 35 years, loving mother of two, and proud grandmother of one. She has penned two books, including the award-winning *Be Brave in the Scared*, recognized by the Association of Catholic Publishers, and has had her work published in seven other books. She is also an acclaimed international speaker, leading transformative retreats for women and presenting conference keynotes. Mary, together with her husband, hosts the popular *Mary and Jerry Podcast*, which enlightens listeners on faith, family, marriage, and much more. Recognized for her captivating speaking style, Mary has a knack for discussing challenging topics with palpable passion and a dash of humor, ensuring her listeners feel seen, acknowledged, and loved by God.

MARIE LOESEL

Marie Loesel is a wife, momma of four littles, and homemaker with a heart for inspiring other mothers to grow in their relationship with the Lord through prayer. Marie is the owner of and designer for Abundance of Grace Prints, an online shop for Catholic prayer cards and products that bring Truth, beauty, and goodness into the everyday. In between wrangling littles and running her shop, she has a passion for encouraging others to build up their domestic church, growing her Marian garden with her daughters, and reading about the lives of the saints.